even in the midst of difficult times. She is still reaching women in our community."

—**Debbie Smee**
Director of Women's Ministries
Porterville Church of the Nazarene
Porterville, California

Have you ever felt like you can't make it? That you can't do one more thing other than scream and run for the hills? Judy Scharfenberg knows exactly how you feel, and is ready and waiting to help you find your way out of frustration and into peace. *Secure Families in a Shaky World* is full of easy-to-do tips on how to stabilize yourself and your family in a hectic world. With time-tested suggestions, she offers six steps that will surprise and encourage you. Her book is guaranteed to leave you with that "I can do this!" inspiration.

—**Davalynn Spencer**
Columnist, Educator
Speaker and Author of *Always Before Me*
www.davalynnspencer.com

SECURE FAMILIES IN A SHAKY WORLD

SECURE
FAMILIES
IN A
SHAKY
WORLD

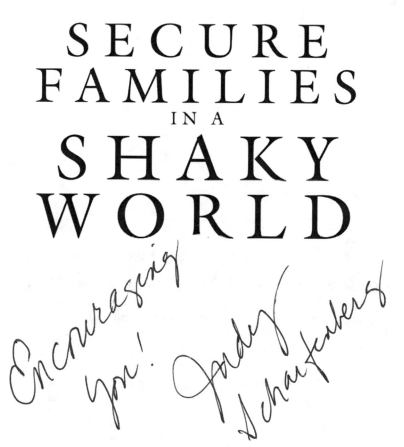

SIX SIMPLE WAYS TO BRING HEALTH AND HOPE
TO YOU, THE HEARTBEAT OF YOUR FAMILY

JUDY SCHARFENBERG

Pleasant Word
A Division of WinePress Group

ISBN 13: 978-1-4141-1529-0
ISBN 10: 1-4141-1529-6
Library of Congress Catalog Card Number: 2009906692

First, I want to dedicate this book to my dear husband, Richard, and my six children: David, Melissa, Jennifer, Andrew, Sarah, and Amy. Without you there would have been no family, no reason to grow, learn, love, and give. You, dear ones, have given me reason for living and have helped me be the best, wife, mom, and grandma I know how to be.

To my prayer partners: Amy, Claudia, Connie, Debbie, Edna, Glenda, Jennifer, Julie, Kim, Lois, Melissa, Nancy, Sarah and Tracy. You have faithfully prayed for my ministry for over fifteen years. We are daughters, sisters, and friends—cogs in a wheel where one speaks, another writes, one prays, another advises, one encourages, another supports and inspires. We are one, and I would be nothing without you.

CONTENTS

INTRODUCTION

D O YOU EVER feel insignificant? Maybe you think you don't matter to your family or friends? I know; it's easy to get down on yourself. You try and try to keep up. And when you can't, you tell yourself, *I'm a complete failure. Why can't I do better? I should be a pro by now.* You get in a rut, and you can't climb out. Days go by without a laugh, a giggle, or even a smile.

Well, let's stop that. I want you to realize that you matter—to your family, to your friends, and most importantly, to God.

Now, there's a reason for your low self-esteem. I've been teaching, counseling, and advising women for over twenty years, and I can tell you that many women are sleep-deprived, frustrated, fearful, frenzied, overcommitted, overwrought, overwhelmed, depressed, and discouraged. Often we feel helpless and resign ourselves to one thought; *It's no use. Life is hard and there's nothing I can do about it.* Some of you have serious difficulties, and the last thing on your mind is feeling important. It's easy to get discouraged.

I know. I've been there.

Sally Field recently said, "Motherhood is given the brush-off in our society. Being a mom is everything. It's mentorship, it's inspirational and it's our hope for the future. I want to applaud moms publicly."[1] I do too. In fact, I want you to applaud yourselves. That may require making a few changes, but I know you're interested. It's why you picked up this book.

Barbara Bush is a wise woman. She's been quoted many times, but the quote I like best is this one: "You have two choices in life. You can like it or not. I chose to like it." Dear one, I want you to like your life.

I spoke at a Mother's Day tea. Afterward a woman came up to me and said, "You know, when you began speaking I thought, *Yeah, right! Another lady born with a Bible in her hand whose life has been perfect, and she's going to tell me how to be happy.* But after I heard your story, I can see that you're just like the rest of us."

I am not a super mom, nor do I have a college degree. What I *do* have is a lifetime of experience. I have been a high school dropout; a pregnant teen; a teenage wife and mom; a single parent who worked full-time; a woman who struggled with alcohol, fear, and depression; a stay-at-home mom; a working mom; and a wife for thirty-eight years. Now I am caregiver for my husband, who suffered a stroke eleven years ago, and mother of six adult children, five of whom are married. I'm also a grandmother of thirteen beautiful darlings—and I'm still counting.

This book is not rocket science. It presents a back-to-basics approach, something we've lost touch with in our fast-paced world. From experience, I can tell you that there's a lot you can do to ensure that your home is fertile soil for a growing, happy, healthy family. I will share with you six simple ways you can begin today that will get you headed in the right direction. These six techniques will create a secure foundation that will give you stability through your toughest trials.

Do you know what will happen? Along the way you're going to look better, feel better, and perhaps even live longer. You're going to find the joy, peace, and security that have eluded you for so long. I'm living proof that *a secure family begins with you and me*.

Before we begin, let me say this. You are always going to see and hear about others who look like they're doing great and lofty things. Don't dwell on their success and don't envy them. People let you see what they want you to see. You do your "stuff" each day, big and little, and I promise—you're going to be headed in the right direction.

Are you ready? Then dig in. This book is for you.

CHAPTER 1

. . . .

SO WHAT'S THE
PROBLEM?

O N A CURRENT TV ad an attractive woman tells us about her long commute to work each day. She says she struggles to take care of herself and her family. She tries to find the best ways to give them what they need—a healthy, energetic, and refreshed wife and mom. She endorses a certain product and with a big smile on her face tells us her world is OK now because of it.

I know she's just trying to sell someone's product, and a few women may be like this smiling lady on TV. But I can't help thinking about most of us who aren't at all like her.

You know what I'm talking about. It's one of those days. You just got home from work. Your husband is working late and won't be home for hours. Or perhaps you're a single parent, the head of your family. You're frantic to put dinner on the table, get your son to karate, and help your daughter with her math homework. The rest of the week looks the same. It's soccer season, and your son has practice twice a week while your daughter babysits regularly for a neighborhood family.

I know. All of you have full schedules. You wish you could just kick off your shoes and sit down for a cup of coffee.

Instead you shove in a load of wash and scribble a few checks for those bills that have been piling up. You don't know if there's enough money in the bank to cover them all. It's a helpless feeling, and you tell yourself, *This is too much. How on earth can we continue this pace? This is not what I planned for my family.*

It's a long night.

From the beginning God has always had the perfect plan for our peace, our contentment, our security—and yes, even our joy. He knows what is good for us. He says, "A joyful heart is good medicine" (Prov. 17:22). And you're thinking, *A joyful heart? Yeah, right.*

Do you remember David, the young boy with the slingshot who killed the giant, Goliath? He grew up to be King David, and along the way he experienced great tragedy and sorrow in his life. He was persecuted. He was hunted like an animal. He even hid in caves. Later, the death of his infant son brought an especially dark time in his life, yet do you know what he wrote about God in the Psalms? "You will make known to me the path of life; In Your presence is fullness of joy; In Your right hand there are pleasures forever" (Ps. 16:11).

You see, the Lord is the Author of joy. He made a way so we would not despair. He knows that even in the midst of turmoil and sorrow we can experience great joy. If Jesus lives in our hearts, then He helps us cope, He helps us see life differently, and He helps us take our eyes off ourselves and focus on the important things. He gives us a plan that's worth following. Sometimes the things that burden us are weights God has placed in our lives so we won't miss Him.

SO WHAT'S THE PROBLEM?

Now, how do we go through this busy life without missing Him? Well, I'm going to give you tools that will help you manage your time, show you what's important, and give you a fresh perspective. The result will be a boost in your confidence, your security, and your peace. Yes, you may even enjoy a laugh or two. You're going to be able to cope with things you never thought possible.

In the next few pages, I'm going to tell you how you can possess a secure family in this shaky world we live in. By definition, your family may be a husband and wife, a single-parent family, a blended family, or a multigenerational family (with grandparents living in the home). Whatever your family is, you'll learn important tips that will help you be a better parent, a better grandparent, or a better aunt, sister or friend.

I'm not perfect, and I'll be the first to say that I wish I could go back and do some things over again. But I don't have a head of gray hair for nothing. Let me share simple ways to help you keep your family secure in this shaky world.

. . . .

CHAPTER 2

THE DINNER TABLE—WHERE CONNECTION IS CREATED

"The wise woman builds her house, but the foolish one tears it down with her own hands."

—Proverbs 14:1

WHEN MY SIX kids were young, our family ate together at the dinner table almost every night. This practice wasn't necessarily by design; we simply couldn't afford to eat out. My father-in-law always said, "You're either rich, or you have kids." A friend recently told me that her family saved at least $500 per month by not eating out. I can believe it.

I didn't realize it then, but I think those dinner hours were the best part of our day. Oh, sometimes we had to rush to a rehearsal here or a practice there, but most evenings we ate together at the table.

Define the Problem

What does dinnertime look like at your house? Are you running in twenty-five different directions by trying to get to this and that? Maybe all of you eat at the counter while standing up. Or maybe you're gulping down food and yelling for everyone to hurry up and get in the car.

I see it in so many lives. Families who don't have time to eat at home are eating their dinner hurriedly in the car while on their way to yet another commitment. Unfortunately, life has changed, and families have lost an important connection with each other. It's true that regular family meals together have all but disappeared from many homes.

Because life is fragile, we must handle it with care. Our families need to connect, and having dinner together is one way to make that connection happen. During a meal, family members bond, children learn to communicate, and everyone feels closer to each other. Meals may be the only times our families pray together. During mealtime you may learn new things about your child that you might not have known otherwise. Studies show that parents who decide that their families will eat together show children that they are important. Children who eat dinner with their families also get better grades. I can't say it enough: dinnertime should be where the family comes together as a team to get support, to provide encouragement, and to be built up and energized.

Emily Bazelon, senior editor of *Slate Magazine* on the Web, says, "The family dinner helps prevent teenagers from abusing drugs or smoking, and it protects them from stress, asthma and eating disorders. It boosts kids' reading scores and grades."[2] Do you want to give your kids the best possible start? Dinner together is a good place to begin.

Connections may take place at meals other than dinner. For some the ideal time may be breakfast or lunch. When two of my grandchildren, Todd and Hannah, were young, their dad worked late as a loan officer. However, he made it a point to come home for lunch, and that's when their family sat down together. Whatever meal you choose can be table time for your family.

The idea of having a meal together may sound overwhelming to you. You may be asking yourself, *how am I going to do this?* This goal won't happen by itself, but with a little planning you can do it.

Getting Started

As you begin, you may experience some resistance. Ask each family member how many nights he or she can gather together. Your younger children, of course, will be more receptive since you can tell them how things are going to be. Some older children may be more challenging; we all know that to them *change* is a bad word. They are going to resist your plans; you can count on it.

I say this: beg, bribe, and bargain. Do whatever it takes. Ask them to just try it for a trial period, say two weeks or so. Then *you* make sure those are the best two weeks at the table they've ever experienced. Hopefully your plans will woo them over, and they won't want to stop.

Making a Plan

Do you get up in the morning and have no idea what you're going to fix for dinner? Maybe you go to the grocery store every day and buy what you need for the evening meal, or maybe you're like my friend Ruth, who stops at a grocery store on her way home from work and picks up a few things.

I know about that; I've been there.

Dinner at the table may take a different direction than you're used to, but once you begin, you're going to wonder why you never tried it before. Below are a few tips that will make getting started even easier.

- **Regular Shopping**

Avoid impulse shopping. My husband was once getting paid every two weeks, so that's when I shopped for
groceries—every two weeks. I waited until evening or the
weekend to do my shopping so whiny, hungry children
weren't tagging along with me. Leaving the kids at home
may not be possible for you every time, but try to go
shopping alone as often as you can. You'll whiz through the
store with much less frustration, and you'll be free from the
pressure to get dinner on the table. With those little ones
not with you, begging for a treat, you'll probably spend less
money as well.

- **Be Prepared**

I always went to the store prepared beforehand. First,
I made a menu of meals that would last twelve days. This
plan actually provided meals for fourteen days and more
because of leftovers. From that menu I made my grocery
list. I often made my menu from the specials in the paper.
With coupons I saved even more.

Normally I didn't buy anything that wasn't on my list. I did
my best to avoid impulse shopping and chose only in-season
fruits and vegetables. When I returned home, I had everything
I needed to prepare those meals for twelve days.

Shopping every two weeks saved me precious time and
money and spared me needless frustration. It requires a little
more thought and planning, but you will experience pure
freedom when you wake each morning knowing that you
have everything on hand for the meal you want to make
that evening. You may need to make a few trips for milk and
produce, but those trips will be short and sweet. This plan
is a real money saver because you are shopping wisely.

- *Compare and Learn*

  I have a friend whose pantry is stuffed. She spends hundreds of dollars whether she needs to or not. Now, this method is OK if you live in the outback and can only get to the store every six months. But my friend goes to the grocery store every week even though there is food at home she's forgotten about. She'll never get to the back of her cupboards, and if she does, everything will be out of date.

- *Plan Ahead*

  When you make your list, choose meats or other proteins you can use for several meals. A store-bought rotisserie chicken, for example, can be shredded and used for several dishes such as enchiladas, chicken tortilla soup, or chicken salad. Slow-cooked pork tenderloin can double as an entrée like barbecued pork sandwiches with just a bottle of barbecue sauce. Cooked beans can go in salad, tacos, and vegetable soup.

  Chop all your vegetables, fruits, and herbs required for a week's meals at one time so everything will be ready for cooking. To avoid a morning rush at breakfast, set your table the night before. It takes just a minute or two to put bowls, utensils, cereal, fruit, toaster, and bread out. How encouraging to wake up to that organization! Your day will start out great.

  Your day will look even better if you pack tomorrow's lunches while preparing dinner. You can hop off to bed knowing you have everything under control. A relaxed mom in the morning is a great gift to your children.

Keeping It Simple

Because my daughters have turned into some pretty good cooks, I love going to their homes for a meal. I can't believe the gourmet meals they turn out, but they never learned those from me. I feel tired when I look at the work required. When they were little, we ate quick-and-easy meals like fried chicken, tacos, spaghetti, tuna casserole, chicken and rice, meat loaf with baked potatoes, or macaroni and cheese. Maybe that's why my girls turned into such gourmet cooks— the food was just too ordinary around our house. But guess what they beg for when they come to my house to eat? Homemade macaroni and cheese!

At the end of this chapter, you'll find five of my easiest recipes. I've also included a grocery list for the meals with all the ingredients to prepare them. Even today I make these meals for company and potlucks, and now everyone thinks *I'm* the gourmet cook.

Shopping Wisely

Feeding a family today demands a major portion of one's budget. It's not easy, but with a little planning you can shave off a few dollars. Here are some cost-saving tips:

- Use meat sparingly. Instead of steak, buy extra lean and cheaper cuts. Cook in a soup or stew in the Crock-Pot.
- Consider adding bean-based meals for dinner. Meals could include burritos, bean soup, or rice and beans. Experiment with a few spices and they'll beg for more.
- Canned meats such as salmon, tuna, chicken, or clams are excellent in pasta and rice dishes, wraps, and casseroles.
- Crock-Pot meals are a great way to tenderize inexpensive meats and tough cuts of meat.

- Stockpile items when you see a good sale.
- Provide less-expensive snacks such as raisins (buy in bulk), popcorn (pop yourself, don't microwave, it's more expensive), carrot sticks, pretzels, cheese, and bananas.

Think Creatively

On some nights you may not have time to put a meal together. When this occurs, stop on the way home from wherever you are and pick up some burgers or chicken. The point is that your family is eating together. By the way, if you know dinner will be late, turn your oven on and place an onion slice inside on a piece of foil. The house will smell like something delicious is cooking, and the aroma will hold off your hungry crowd until you get dinner on the table. This really works. Just make sure you offer a good meal eventually.

My son, David, is a great cook and somehow finds time to cook even though both he and his wife, Kris, work full-time. Often Kris sets a Crock-Pot meal to cook before she heads out the door in the morning. Because David gets home before Kris does, he makes a salad, sets the table, and pours the beverages. When Kris walks in, he greets her with a hug and kiss, and they sit down for dinner. Now that's teamwork.

Table Topics

My husband created the ABC Game. We go around the table, and each person says a biblical name for letters in the alphabet: starting with A for Adam, B for Barnabas, C for Cyrus, D for Daniel, and so on. With eight of us, the game is a real challenge. Felix and Festus are names we might never have known had we never played this game. The game can became very competitive, but it's always fun. Try using the names of capital cities or states.

Other table topics include asking your kids about their day at school. Don't ask them what they did. They're going to say, "Nothing." Instead ask them, "What did your teacher read to you today?" or "Who did you have lunch with?"

You could designate one night as "joke night." Remind family members in the morning about the special theme so they can be prepared to bring their best jokes. It's important that family members respect each other and not interrupt. The rule is that you must laugh even if the joke is corny. Here's a joke to get you started. "What do you call a fairy who needs a bath? 'Stinker Bell.'" Little ones can get involved more than you think. My five-year-old grandson, Connor, asked his dad, "Why did the cookie go to the doctor? His precocious smile was precious as he quipped, "Because he felt crummy!"

So there you go. A quick Internet search will provide a dozen games, jokes and ideas that will be fun for your family as you sit down together at the table for family mealtime.

Dr. Phil McGraw is committed to preserving the family. In his book, Family First, he affirms the importance of families having dinner together. His suggestion at mealtime is to ask each member to describe two good things or bad things that happened that day. He says, "This is an excellent way for family members to open themselves up to one another, and it serves to bring everyone closer."[3] What a terrific way to encourage each family member, showing them how to give and receive praise and compassion. We all need encouragement, our children most of all.

William Arthur Ward said, "Flatter me, and I may not believe you. Criticize me, and I may not like you.

a

Ignore me, and I may not forgive you. Encourage me, and I will not forget you. Love me and I may be forced to love you."[4] Your kids may not remember what they had for dinner, but they will remember your encouraging dinnertime talks.

Don't Stop There

Another tip that will help you and those you know is to start a monthly meal exchange program. Once a month, cook enough food for two dinners. Stash one in the freezer and give the other to a friend or neighbor. Go one step further and organize an exchange with four or five friends. Each of you will collect five meals to take home. Voilà! Including the meal you just put in the freezer, you'll have a whole week of healthy, ready-to-cook main dishes. On a hectic night, pop one in the oven, and you're all set.

Finally, designate thirty minutes after dinner for cleanup. Don't forget to include your kids in chores. You need to teach them, they want to learn, and they'll enjoy helping, especially after they receive all the praise you're going to give them. Get everyone involved in clearing away clutter, wiping the table, rinsing dishes, loading the dishwasher, and taking the trash out. You will not only get the help you need and cut cleanup time in half but also teach your family members valuable skills that will carry over into their adulthood.

More Ways to Cultivate Character and Family Relationships

1. Memorize Psalm 1 as a family.
2. Write each family member a letter, sharing why you value that person.

3. Put a 500-piece jigsaw puzzle together.
4. Spend an hour playing with your children. Let them choose the activity.
5. Take your teenager out for breakfast. Listen to him or her.
6. As a family, help serve Thanksgiving dinner at a homeless shelter or invite to your home someone who would otherwise be spending Thanksgiving Day alone.
7. Make sure you have given each child clearly defined chores. Teach your daughters how to cut the grass and your sons how to clean the floors.
8. To the best of your ability, give affirming words to your children during the first and last five minutes of each day.
9. Children consistently study better, sleep better, and generally enjoy life better without distractions in their bedroom, for example: television, computers and video gaming systems.
10. Get everyone involved in setting the Sunday morning breakfast table on Saturday night.
11. Buy a medal from an army surplus store. Declare it to be your family's "medal of courage." When one of your children does something courageous, make a big deal out of the accomplishment at dinnertime. Let the child wear the medal for a day or two.
12. Plant and maintain a garden together.
13. Don't hesitate to plan a party for no reason.
14. Ask your children to select toys, books, games, and clothes they have outgrown. As a family, donate items to the Salvation Army or to a family who needs them.

FIVE EASY RECIPES

1. Chicken Divan

2 lbs. cooked chicken, cut into bite-sized pieces
2 cans cream of chicken soup
1 cup mayonnaise
1 Tbsp. curry powder (more or less, depending on taste)
1 cup shredded cheddar cheese
1 lb. bag of frozen broccoli florets, cooked and drained

1. Layer broccoli and chicken in a rectangular baking dish.
2. Mix together soup (*do not add water*), mayonnaise, and curry powder. Spread mixture on top of chicken and broccoli.
3. Top with shredded cheddar cheese.
4. Bake at 350 degrees for 35–45 minutes. Keep your eye on it!

Makes eight servings. Serve over steamed rice. Include a green salad and cranberry sauce or a gelatin salad. (Jell-O® and fruit cocktail) A dinner roll completes the meal.

2. Swiss Steak (Crock-Pot Meal)

2 or 3 lbs. top round steak, cut into pieces
1 medium onion, sliced (You can also add fresh sliced mushrooms and bell pepper.)
2 cans golden mushroom soup

1. Place steak pieces in Crock-Pot; add sliced onion, mushrooms, and bell pepper.
2. Spread golden mushroom soup on top (*do not add water*).
3. Cover and cook on Low 6–8 hours. You might take a peek in the middle and stir really well one time.

Makes eight servings. Serve over cooked white rice or noodles. Add mixed vegetables and cornbread to complete your easy meal.

3. South-of-the-Border Lasagna

1 lb. ground turkey
2 cans crushed or diced tomatoes
1 cup picante sauce
1 pkg. taco seasoning mix
½ cup diced green chilies
1 cup ricotta cheese
9 cooked lasagna noodles (whole wheat noodles makes this a healthier meal)
4 oz. grated Parmesan cheese

1. Brown turkey; add tomatoes, picante sauce, taco mix, and chilies.
2. Simmer ten minutes.
3. In bottom of nine-inch pan, layer a little sauce, noodles, ricotta, and rest of sauce. End with sauce. Sprinkle with Parmesan cheese.
4. Bake 20–30 minutes at 350 degrees.

Makes eight servings. With a salad, bread, and butter, you'll have a meal everyone will enjoy.

4. Super Easy Chicken Tortilla Soup (Crock-Pot Meal)

4–6 chicken breasts, cut into chunks
1 can black beans
1 box Zattaran's red beans and rice mix
1 can corn

Half an onion, chopped
2 cans chicken broth
2 cans water
1 cup favorite salsa or picante sauce
1 tbs. cumin

1. Cook chicken, chopped onion, and cumin in salsa in pan on stovetop.
2. Combine chicken broth, water, black beans, and corn (do not drain or rinse beans or corn) into Crock-Pot.
3. Cook the Zattaran's beans and rice mix separately according to package directions.
4. When chicken is done, add it to the Crock-Pot. When the beans and rice mix is done, add that too.
5. Let it cook all day. The longer it cooks, the better it tastes! Garnish with tortilla strips, cheese, cilantro, sliced green onions, sour cream, and avocado—whatever sounds good. Makes eight servings.

5. Seasoned Turkey Meatballs

2 lbs. ground turkey
1 onion, grated
1 egg
¾ cup seasoned bread crumbs
Salt and pepper
½ cup butter or margarine
3 tbs. all-purpose flower
1 cup milk
1 cup water

1. In large bowl combine first four ingredients and 1 tsp. salt. Shape into one-inch meatballs.
2. In skillet on low heat, melt butter.

3. Brown meatballs on all sides. Remove meatballs. Stir in flour, pepper, and 1 tsp. salt.
4. Gradually stir in milk and water. Heat to boiling, stirring to loosen bits from skillet.
5. Return meatballs to skillet. Heat to boiling. Reduce heat to Low. Cover and simmer ten minutes, stirring occasionally.

Makes eight servings. Serve over white rice. Your favorite vegetable or green salad will finish this meal beautifully.

These five meals will stretch into six, maybe seven, depending on leftovers. Here is a grocery list of all the items you will need to prepare these meals. The best idea is to prepare your weekly menu after checking your newspaper ads for specials. Clipping coupons will help you save at the register.

Grocery List for Five Easy Recipes

1 can black beans
1 can corn
2 cans chicken broth
2 cans diced tomatoes
1 large can diced green chilies
2 cans cream of chicken soup
2 cans golden mushroom soup
1 can cranberry sauce
1 jar mayonnaise
1 large jar picante sauce
1 pkg. taco seasoning mix
1 can Parmesan cheese
1 box Zattaran's red beans and rice
1 pkg. lasagna noodles
2 lb. pkg. rice

1 pkg. noodles
1 box Jell-O®, raspberry or strawberry
1 can fruit cocktail
Seasoned bread crumbs
Salad dressing, your choice of flavor
1 pkg. corn bread mix
1 bag tortilla strips
1 loaf French bread
1 pkg. dinner rolls

Garlic powder   Ricotta cheese
Basil leaves   2 lbs. cheddar cheese
Oregano leaves   Sour cream
Cumin powder   Butter, eggs, milk
Curry powder   1 pkg. of frozen broccoli
1 pkg. frozen mixed vegetables

5 lbs. boneless chicken breasts
3–4 lbs. ground turkey
3 lbs. top round steak

Various lettuces or bagged salad mixtures
Tomatoes, avocados, green onions
Cilantro, onions, celery
Fresh mushrooms, bell pepper

The Dinner Table—Where Connection Is Created

Get ready! Reflect: What do my habits—good and bad—look like?

How are they working for me?

Get set! Pray and plan: Is there something I should change?

Go! Take action: What's the first step? When will I begin?

Competition for family time is fierce. Whether it's a game at dinner or a prayer at breakfast, make connections your top priority. If mealtime is fun and interesting, your home will be an optimum learning environment, and your family will clamor for more.

Prayer

Father, help me to be creative and persistent. I want to generate an atmosphere that will encourage, support, build up, and energize my family. We want to stay connected. In Jesus' name, amen.

CHAPTER 3

· ·

THE READING CIRCLE—WHERE CHARACTER IS INTRODUCED

"Repeat them again and again to your children. Talk about them when you are at home and when you are away on a journey, when you are lying down and when you are getting up again."

—Deuteronomy 6:7 NLT

E
VERYWHERE WE TURN, another reading incentive program is being advertised. I think we would agree that reading and literacy are important issues today, but that's not the problem. The problem is finding time to read. I'm busy, and you're busy. Life is hectic. My six children are all adults now, but I still remember days filled with loads of laundry, weekly trips to the orthodontists (we had three kids in braces), and allergy clinics.

I know what it's like to have a busy afternoon and evening fixing dinner, cleaning up, giving baths, and then helping with homework. Our children's ages were spread out from newborn to college age. For years, I drove kids to and from elementary school, middle school, and high school. That's thirty trips a week!

I could hardly wait until everyone was in bed so I could have some time to myself. I'd plan to take a leisurely bath or give myself a fresh manicure. But what really happened was that I'd fall asleep on the couch, shuffle off to bed, and settle for a five-minute shower in the morning.

Your life may be just as hectic, yet you've carved out time to read to your family. I applaud you. Maybe you're not a mom, but you know what? A child doesn't mind if Aunt Ellen or a neighbor or a big sister is doing the reading. You could give a busy mom in your life a nice break by reading to her children once in a while.

Reasons Why You Should Read to Your Children

- They will develop their ability to retain a sequence of ideas and build their vocabulary.
- They will learn to listen, and their attention spans will increase.
- You will strengthen your emotional bond with your children.
- You will help your children gain experience in speaking and be more confident in school.
- The best part is that you'll get off your feet for fifteen minutes.

When you read to your children, you'll discover all those benefits and more. You see, learning to read is one of the most important steps your children will ever take. We want to be sure their first experiences with words and books are happy and successful. What better place to be than snuggled at your side? I advise new mothers to start early. Put your baby on your lap and begin with a bright colored board book. He won't understand, but that time on your lap, hearing your voice and feeling your warmth is irreplaceable.

Learning that books are friends and that words have magic will carry into the school years and make a world of difference in years to come. Children who become achievers in school come from homes where parents place importance on reading for pleasure.

A Few Suggestions

Surround children with books and writing. Visit your library regularly and make buying new books a frequent treat. Put cloth and board books near baby and keep one or two books in the car for older children. Children learn to read and love books when adults share their own pleasure in reading. Books fall open, and you fall in.

Things to Avoid

TV, Internet, and video games! We need to limit all these media, but let's focus on TV for now. The amount of time kids spend in front of the TV has a lot to do with how successful they become as readers. When I worked as a children's librarian one of my colleagues, a kindergarten teacher, told me that after talking with parents and their children, she discovered that some of her students had spent over 5,000 hours in front of the TV before they ever began school. That's more time than it takes to earn a university degree!

I know, I know—turning on the TV is so easy to do. You have only so many hours in a day and so much to get done. It can be heaven when your children sit quietly and watch a TV program while you fix dinner. There's nothing really wrong with that either, but the practice can easily get out of hand.

Children who watch a lot of TV aren't learning to reach for books as a source of pleasure. In addition, when young children watch TV, you can't really know if they understand what they see and hear. Many young children barely make sense out of those rapidly changing sights and sounds. When they enter school, they've been so captivated by TV that they struggle to sit and learn for long periods of time in a classroom. They have no remote controls to change the teacher.

Children copy what they see. When you turn off the TV and read a newspaper, a magazine, or a book, your child learns that reading is important.

When I was a school librarian, 650 students visited my library each week to check out books and listen to a story. Sometimes I practically had to do a song and a dance to hold their attentions. Media-saturated children are accustomed to fast-action programs and video games. I could tell that many children were not used to being read to; in fact, some of them even told me they didn't like it. But I chose a captivating story and was very animated as I read it. One of my joys was to watch them settle down and listen intently. They ended up enjoying it. This will happen to you as well.

More Good Tips

- Read daily. If you have a busy schedule, you can read a shorter book, but try to read something every day. Some parents make story reading a bedtime ritual; others include it as part of family times. Some of our best family times were when I read to all my kids together. I remember that one book was the story of John Newton,[5] who wrote the hymn "Amazing

Grace." Amy was nine, and Sarah was eleven. Andrew, who was thirteen, said, "I'm too old to be read to." The funny thing is, each night he scooted a little closer until he was right there with his sisters as if he'd been there all along. They were so captivated by this story that we had to take it with us when we went on vacation.

- A friend told me about a special time after she had an emergency appendectomy (she was twenty-four). Her mother visited her in the hospital and read to her one of her favorite childhood books, *Madeline* by Ludwig Bemelmans. In this story Madeline has her appendix taken out. My friend said that hearing her mom read to her again was a real comfort when she was in such an emotional state.

- You're never too old to be read to. In fact, when a stroke affected my husband's eyesight, I began reading to him each morning. We've just finished *Treasure Island*, a novel he missed during his childhood, and now we're reading *The Scarlet Pimpernel*. I found a condensed version in a Reader's Digest publication.[6] Richard told me it's a bit wordy, but when I ask if I should stop, he says, "No, keep going." I think he likes it.

- Read expressively. Let your voice reflect your enthusiasm for what you're reading so your genuine interest in the story comes through. If you like the story, the children will too. You can add variety and maintain your child's attention if you add some sound effects to the words. For example, "The old door creeeeaked!" or "The wind groooaned!" Children love sound effects. Just be ready for them to imitate you.

- Create excitement by speaking slightly faster. Whisper or pause briefly to add suspense. For example, "'Run! Run!'" Jonathan whispered. "'Just get out of here before you get caught.'"
- Read creatively. Make the story fun. When your children are young, you can read stories, songs, or poems aloud, making a variety of voices for the different characters. Ask your child to join in and help make the noises that go with animals or actions. As your children learn to read for themselves, encourage them to make different voices as they read to you.
- Read it again. Young children thrive on repetition. After your children have become familiar with a story, omit a word and let them fill in the blank. Be careful though if *you* fill in the blank and change the story. I was reading to a friend's child one day, obviously from a book she'd heard often. In the story the family got up on Sunday and went to Grandma's house. I decided it was a good time to insert some religion into the story, so I said, "And they all got up on Sunday *and went to church.*" My little listener glared at me indignantly and said, "They did not!"
- Help your child become an active reader. As you read together, share ideas and ask questions like these: "What do you think will happen next?" "What do you think about the story?" "Did the character do the right thing?" Talking with your children will help build the listening and speaking skills they need to become good readers. As your children get older, ask questions about what they read on their own. When they tell you the story, they are learning to remember information and organize it.
- Follow the story with fun-to-do activities. Discuss how the story characters may have felt and try to

think about how the child might have felt in a similar situation. You might talk about different endings, which is always a good way to think critically and teach your children how to make wise choices.

- Provide art materials for your children to use in drawing or painting a picture of their favorite part of the story. You can buy lined paper that offers enough blank space on the top for a picture to be drawn and a caption about the picture to be written underneath.

- Read all around you. Read everything you see— cereal boxes and T-shirts, road signs and billboards, maps and signs in the grocery store. Help your children see that reading is important in everything they do.

- Always have books on hand. Go to the library every week. It's free and open to everyone. Bring your children to story time or ask the librarian to help your kids choose books catered to their special interests. Children get excited when they can choose from hundreds of books. If you can't get to the library, see if a bookmobile stops near you. Ask your children to bring home books from the school library. Shop at garage sales and encourage books as gifts.

- Give books as gifts to the children in your life, but go one step further. If you give a little one the popular *If You Give a Mouse a Cookie* by Laura Numeroff, include an apron, a box of cookie mix, and a wooden spoon. A book is a present you can give again and again.

- Thrift stores are also wonderful places to buy books. I have found like-new, popular, hardbound children's books for fifty cents. Do the footwork, and it won't take long for you to build your child's library.

Expect Great Results

"Read some more!" is one of the highest compliments your listeners can give you, and I hope you hear those words many times. For more help in reading, I suggest *The Read-Aloud Handbook* by Jim Trelease, a favorite resource for parents and librarians. Another favorite is *Honey for a Child's Heart* by Gladys Hunt. In both books you'll find tips, advice, and lists of excellent books to read.

The Bible says, "And do not be conformed to this world, but be transformed by the renewing of your mind" (Rom. 12:2). You can renew minds in a grand way when you choose good books to read to your children.

Winston Churchill said, "You make a living by what you earn. You make a life by what you give." Never underestimate the power you have to change a life. God has placed you in your child's life for a reason. You will touch that little life in ways you may not realize until later. I hope you'll look at reading to your child as one important way.

Our Family's Favorite Read-Aloud Books

Grade Three and Up

Treasures of the Snow by Patricia St. John
Annette's little brother is crippled, and Lucien, the village bully, is responsible. Angry and hateful, Annette vows she will never forgive Lucien and sets out to hurt him.

The Best Christmas Pageant Ever by Barbara Robinson
In this annual favorite the rowdy Herdman family takes over the church Christmas pageant.

Family Tree by Katherine Ayers
Readers will get caught up in eleven-year-old Tyler's personal story of family differences and secrets and by her quest for the grandparents she has never known. Fascinating facts about the Amish culture will hold the reader's interest (1999 California Young Reader Medal winner).

Martin the Cobbler, adapted from a fable by Leo Tolstoy
Good for the whole family, this story illustrates the Scripture beautifully. "For I was hungry, and you gave Me something to eat; I was thirsty, and you gave Me something to drink; I was a stranger, and you invited Me in ... You did it to Me" (Matt. 25:35, 40).

The Pinballs by Betsy Byars
Three unwanted kids collide in a warm, caring foster home and learn about love, respect, and compassion as they pin their hopes and dreams on each other and on their foster parents.

Understood Betsy by Dorothy Canfield Fisher
Timid Elizabeth is sent to live with distant relatives in Vermont. This old, tender story is about a child's awakening to self and others.

My Father's Dragon by Ruth Stiles Gannett and Ruth Chrisman Gannett
This Newbery Honor Book from 1948 is still a favorite today. This humorous adventure story is about a boy who

uses his wits to rescue an enslaved baby dragon. The three books in this series have delighted children and their parents for generations.

Mrs. Piggle-Wiggle by Betty Bard MacDonald
    This series of stories is about a remarkable old lady whom children love because she lives in an upside-down house, smells like cookies, and was once married to a pirate.

Roll of Thunder, Hear My Cry by Mildred D. Taylor
    This is a story about a black family's struggle in Mississippi during the Depression. Seen through the eyes of a nine-year-old, this story won the Newbery Medal.

The Tower of Geburah by John White (teens and mature readers)
    Children are involved in a struggle against good and evil. Highly recommended. My daughter Amy will tell you this was her absolute favorite.

John Newton, the Angry Sailor by Kay Marshall Strom
    This is the true story of John Newton, the author of our beloved hymn, Amazing Grace. John hated being a sailor, had a horrible life at sea, being whipped and mistreated. He became one of the worst slave traders ever. Read how God miraculously changed his life.

Little Pilgrim's Progress by Helen L. Taylor
    Christian's pilgrimage is a story of adventure. Helen L. Taylor has simplified the story for younger readers. The result is a classic for youth, a delightful book with a message they can understand. One of my children's favorites.

THE READING CIRCLE—
WHERE CHARACTER IS INTRODUCED

The Chronicles of Narnia by C. S. Lewis
    Deceptively simple and direct, *The Chronicles of Narnia* continue to captivate fans with adventures, characters, and truths that speak to readers of all ages.

The Reading Circle—Where Character Is Introduced

Get ready! Reflect: What do my habits—good and bad—look like?

How are they working for me?

Get set! Pray and plan: Is there something I should change?

Go! Take action: What's the first step? When will I begin?

Story time is another way to connect.. Fifteen minutes with your children will fulfill a great need in their lives. This single activity will strengthen your emotional closeness, showing them how important they are to you.

Prayer

Lord, help me to understand the priority You place on children. Thank You for these precious gifts. Reading to them is one way we can stay close. Help me to develop a plan, make it my priority, and stick with it. In Jesus' name, amen.

CHAPTER 4

THE VOLUNTEER SQUAD—WHERE JOY IS DISCOVERED

"….He who is gracious to the needy, honors Him."
—Proverbs 14:31

THE BIBLE SAYS, "Do nothing from selfishness or empty conceit, but with humility of mind let each of you regard one another as more important than himself; do not merely look out for your own personal interests, but also for the interests of others."[7] Why is that? It's simple really. A lot of people need our help.

Expect the Unexpected

A good friend of mine came home from work one day and found her husband lying on the floor, dead from a heart attack. Naturally, her life was shattered, and it's taken a long time for her to get back to the living. Another friend talked her into volunteering at her local hospital. She went reluctantly.

You should see her now. She reads to patients and writes letters for them. Sometimes she just listens to them. She's a really funny gal, and most of the time she brings smiles to their faces. Susan is a happy woman again, and she feels like her life has meaning and purpose. It's really true that when we give ourselves to others, we will feel better.

Everyone loves to give at Thanksgiving and Christmas. We listen to those beautiful carols about peace on earth and good will toward men. We get busy, bake our cookies and pumpkin bread, and visit the hospitals. (Did you know that hospitals experience more visitors in December than at any other time of the year?) We tell ourselves, "This is great. I'm going to do this more often." But the holidays pass, we get back into our routines, and somehow we just can't fit it all in.

I heard about an eighty-five-year-old man who shopped at a Kroger store in Georgia. Described as "sort of a mean old man" and "bossy and very particular about things," he ate breakfast in the store each morning. Sometimes on hot summer days, he didn't bother wearing a shirt or shoes. He often frowned, grumbled, and commented on how the female clerks in the store were overweight. No one had a good thing to say about this fellow.

The old man died of cancer. A few weeks later, another man entered the store and began handing out $10,000 checks to several of the clerks. A financial advisor for the old man, he explained that his client had gotten to know the ladies pretty well and thought they could probably use the money. What had they done to merit such a gift? *They had talked to him!*

In 1 Peter 3: 9-10 9, we're told "To sum up, let all be harmonious, sympathetic, brotherly, kindhearted, and humble in spirit; not returning evil for evil, or insult for insult, but giving a blessing instead; for you were called for the very purpose that you might inherit a blessing." The Bible also says that the proper use of our words is "like apples of gold in settings of silver" (Prov. 25:11). People need a tender touch. Did you know that babies who are held grow faster? That the touch of a hand lowers blood pressure? That a smile releases good hormones in our bodies and generally causes others to smile back?

Kind Words Make a Difference

You and I are going to cross paths with people who are hot-tempered, disgruntled, and impatient. We can turn their bad day into a good one with a kind word and a smile. We may not get a $10,000 check, but the reward will be better than that. The good feelings we get from doing someone a good turn is worth a million bucks.

Dale Carnegie said, "You may forget tomorrow the kind words you said today, but the recipient will cherish them for a lifetime." I'll bet someone comes to your mind right now, someone who changed your life with a kind word and a smile.

I heard about a woman who always went to a specific branch post office in her town because the postal employees were friendly. On one busy afternoon, she stopped by to purchase a few stamps. While waiting in the long line, a man pointed out that she didn't need to wait; she could get her stamps at the machine in the lobby. "I know," she said, "but the machine won't ask me about my arthritis!"

Little Things Mean a Lot

In a more tangible way you could organize a volunteer housecleaning group to go out every other week or once a month to somebody who needs you. Call a friend out of the blue and pray with her. Provide a meal for someone who is ill. Drive someone to the grocery store and help with shopping, or shop for her if she's unable to. Bring your neighbor's trash cans in. If you keep your eyes and ears open, you'll find ways to give to others in no time.

At my recent garage sale, my neighbor came over to see what I had for sale. Naturally, I greeted him and asked how he was doing. "Not so good," he replied. "My brother-in-law committed suicide the other day."

I was stunned, speechless really. "Nate, I'm so sorry," I murmured. He wanted to talk, and I listened. He went home looking so sad. My heart went out to him, but I didn't know what to do. Later, I impulsively bought a bouquet of flowers, stuck them in a vase, made some brownies, put them on a pretty plate, and delivered the flowers and brownies to Nate and his wife. Along life's road, you and I will meet plenty of hurting people. We may not know exactly what to say or do, but we need to reach out any way we can. Nate and his wife know that I care, and I'm hoping that simple act will build our friendship.

Be Creative

My hairdresser, Deborah, married with two children, confessed that she doesn't know how to cook. When I asked what she does for dinner, she replied that they eat a lot of baked chicken. I think her husband throws most of their meals together. Last Christmas I gave her two of my favorite recipes (listed at the end of Chapter Two). Then I fixed a pretty basket containing all the nonperishable items she'd need to prepare those meals.

The next time I saw her, she couldn't thank me enough. "My husband just loved those recipes," she said. "He took leftovers to work for three days." A recipe care package is a great gift for busy young moms, wedding showers, and just anytime gifts. When I give this message to a group of women, one of the door prizes is a basket of recipes and ingredients. Women have told me that the basket is one of the best gifts they've ever received. It's practical and useful, it gives them a fresh idea, and it shows that you really care.

For several years now, I have been packing meals in bags with nonperishable items like granola bars, canned fruit with pop-top lids, pork and beans, Vienna sausages, boxed fruit juice, bottled water, packaged cheese and crackers, a plastic spoon and napkin, and a little Scripture tract. When homeless people ask me for money, I hand them one of the bags, and then I pray for them. I tell the Lord, "I've given them some physical food and some spiritual food, Lord. Use Your Word to touch their lives."

Include Your Family

Your kids could help you pack the bags. When they see mom and dad giving, they will become givers too. My last child at home has seen me pack these bags, and now she's doing it too. She calls it her "bum food." It has done my heart good to see her pick up on this idea and be a cheerful giver.

When my daughters were teenagers, we baby-sat for mothers who needed to go shopping, especially around the holidays. We fed the kids lunch, played games with them, and put them down for naps. We had a houseful of kids, and it was a busy place, but the experience was so worth it to the moms and to us. I knew from experience what a day of shopping without the kids was like, and this service was a great example for my daughters. You should see them today. All four of my daughters have compassionate, giving hearts, and I just love watching them serve others.

When we visited our daughter Jennifer in Arizona last year, she was furiously wiping up the kitchen, getting an early start on dinner, and preparing a meal to take to a family in her church. She turned to me, pretending to be upset, and said, "Oh no! Mom, I've turned into you."

She can't fool me. I know she was pleased, and you can be sure that her heart of service makes me feel really good too.

Charitable Giving

If you want $50 in authentic happiness, just donate $50 to your favorite charity. People who give to charity are 43 percent more likely than non-givers to say they're very happy. It doesn't matter whether the gifts go to churches or symphony orchestras; religious and secular giving leaves people equally happy and far happier than people who don't give. Even donating blood, an especially personal kind of giving, improves our attitudes. It's easy to see, the more people give, the happier they get.

I bet you can think of someone right now whom God has placed on your heart to reach out to. God wants to use you and me, and you know He takes even the littlest things and makes them big deals. If you have a computer, why not Google volunteering in your area? You'll come up with a multitude of opportunities. Any outreach to show people the love of God is exactly where He knows we will thrive.

I've included some checklists to help get you started. Why not plan on doing one item each week, whether you feel like it or not? In fact, don't stop with these lists. I know you can think of a dozen items to add to it. Make it your way of life, and you know what? Everybody wins!

My Checklist for Joy

- Mend a quarrel; apologize; ask for forgiveness.
- Seek out a forgotten friend.
- Write a long overdue thank you note, maybe to a family member.
- Hug someone tightly and whisper, "I love you."
- Forgive an enemy; pray for him or her.
- Be gentle and patient with an angry person.
- Gladden the heart of a child.
- Find the time to keep a promise.
- Make or bake something for someone else... anonymously.
- Release a grudge; do not let the sun go down on your anger. (Eph. 4:26)
- Listen. Smile.
- Speak kindly to a stranger.
- Take a walk with a friend.
- Plant a garden.
- Kneel down and pet a dog.
- Read to your mate or friend.
- Lessen your demands on others.
- Play some beautiful music during the evening meal.
- Turn off the TV and talk.
- Treat someone to an ice cream cone.
- Give a soft answer when you want to give a hard one.
- Encourage an older person.
- Tell someone how much you appreciate him or her and why.
- Offer to baby-sit for a weary mother.
- Encourage the teachers in your life. (Teachers have told me they have all the candles they will ever need.

Gift certificates to book stores or restaurants will brighten their day.)
- Do the dishes without grumbling; don't even sigh.

More Ideas for Volunteering

- Celebrate your next birthday at your local food bank. Volunteer in the kitchen for a few hours, and then have cake and ice cream with the staff and other volunteers.
- Drive seniors or shut-ins to their doctors' appointments, the library, or the grocery store.
- Perhaps you have small children at home, and finances are tight. You might not be able to get out, but you can call the seniors in your life and chat. Listen carefully; you'll hear about something you can pray for. You will also make their lonely day a lot brighter.
- Finished with your magazines? Don't throw them away. Take them to your local hospital and donate them to the family waiting rooms.
- When there's a sale on deodorant, lotion, or face wash, stock up and then take the items to your local women's shelter. You could even volunteer at the shelter by reading to the children, counseling, working in the kitchen, and so on.
- Remember, adults love being read to as well. I read once a week to the patrons at a stroke activity center. They eagerly looked forward to each session. One of our favorites was *Marley and Me*, by John Grogan.
- Mow lawns and weed gardens for those who can't do it for themselves any longer.
- Many local hospitals accept handmade hats and sweaters for newborn babies to wear home.

- Local animal shelters are always in need of volunteers who love animals.
- Find a church, shelter or some other charity you can all get involved in on a regular basis. Show your children how good it feels to give. They will experience a tremendous sense of accomplishment.

The Volunteer Squad—Where Joy Is Discovered

Get ready! Reflect: What do my habits—good and bad—look like?

How are they working for me?

Get set! Pray and plan: Is there something I should change?

Go! Take action: What's the first step? When will I begin?

Perhaps it's been a while since you've even had time to think about others. Somehow in our fast-paced society, we've lost our connectedness. It's not about us, but about others. God will prompt us, putting on a little pressure, but He will never force us. Putting others first requires daily surrender to ourselves. Why not make this your prayer?

Prayer

"Father, there are people in my life every day who have needs. I've been blinded, thinking only of myself for far too long. Would you open my eyes and help me see the needs around me? May I have Your giving heart, and would You lead me to someone who needs a tender touch? In Jesus' name, amen."

. . . .

CHAPTER 5

THE TREADMILL— WHERE PERSISTENCE IS REWARDED

"…..A tranquil heart is life to the body."
—Proverbs 14:30

I'M COUNSELING A young single woman I'll call Karen. She's fifteen years younger than I am, but if you saw her, you'd think she was older than me. She's listless and tired, and her face is creased with worry lines.

Karen takes care of her aging parents. Her mom is terminally ill, and her dad is disabled. Cranky and verbally abusive to Karen, he has begun shoving her when he gets upset. Karen is unemployed and her car is a clunker. She never knows if it's going to start.

I don't blame her for being overwhelmed, do you? Now, I know it may be hard for her to change her circumstances, but I helped her to see how she might start making changes in herself. First Corinthians 6:19-20 says, "Do you not know that your body is a temple of the Holy Spirit who is in you, whom you have from God, and that you are not your own?

For you have been bought with a price: therefore glorify God in your body" (1 Cor. 6:19–20).

If you are a Christian, then you know that the Holy Spirit lives inside you, His temple. For that reason, we have an obligation to take care of our bodies in the best way we can.

Choices Karen has made may have contributed to her depression. Doctors say that in some cases we can avoid depression and other ailments simply by adding a little exercise to our daily routines.

May I Make a Disclaimer Right Here?

Many cases of serious depression require a doctor's care and sometimes medication. I do not want to make light of a critical situation. When in doubt, please consult your doctor.

Karen told me that when she takes a walk or goes for a swim, she has more energy and is better able to cope with her problems. She faces a vicious cycle, however, because she's always tired and can quickly talk herself out of a walk. I know exactly what she means.

My husband suffered a stroke eleven years ago. Now he sits in a wheelchair and needs me to do many things for him that he used to do for himself. Being a caregiver is a whole new way of life and a big responsibility. For the sake of my husband, I have an obligation to keep myself in good shape. I can tell you honestly that being my husband's caregiver is the *only* reason why I go to the gym to exercise when it's early in the morning and still dark outside.

Frankly, I don't like going to the gym; I like *having gone* to the gym. If you exercise, you know what I'm talking about. It's like pulling teeth to get there. But on the way home—Whoa!—those endorphins are popping around in my brain. I have a long mental list of things to do, and I can hardly wait to get home and get started. I burst into the bedroom where my dear Richard is still sleeping, whip off those covers, and bellow, "Come on, sweetie pie! It's a beautiful day! Time to get up!"

Did you know that sleeping people do not like cheerful people who have just exercised? Sometimes he peeps at me from the slit of one eye and says with all the sarcasm he can muster that early, "You've been to the gym again, haven't you?" One morning he told me, "This is getting more like boot camp every day." He even started calling me "sergeant," but then he added "sweetheart." I can handle Sergeant Sweetheart.

Rosemary Ellis, editor-in-chief of *Good Housekeeping*, agrees with me about exercise. "When I get up early in the morning and go for a walk or a run," she said, "my whole day goes better. Being outdoors then and pushing my body seems to pull the rip cord on all the bundled-up stress my brain has been storing up. Solutions to knotty problems magically materialize. I get a head start on my day."[8]

You've heard the saying "If Mama ain't happy, ain't nobody happy." You and I know that it's true. Exercise will energize you and change your attitude. You're going to laugh more, and when you do, it'll come right back at you. If there's one thing we need more of in our lives, it's laughter.

What Does Laughter Have to Do with It?

I recently spoke with Dr. William Fry, professor emeritus at the Stanford University School of Medicine. He has studied humor for over fifty years. He told me, "Mirthful laughter is a quick mood changer that can erase fear, anger, anxiety and depression. From a physical standpoint, we've learned that laughter conditions the heart muscle, exercises the lungs and diaphragm, works all of the abdominal and thoracic muscles, boosts the immune system and even increases the adrenaline and blood flow to the brain."[9]

A colleague of Dr. Fry's is Dr. Lee Berk, a pioneer researcher and professor studying positive emotions and their biochemical and physiological effects at Loma Linda University School of Medicine in California. He said "Laughter increases alertness, creativity and pain tolerance. It lowers blood pressure and it improves respiration. Simply put, it helps you breathe easier." [10]

Don't you find this amazing? God is a genius. No wonder He says, "A joyful heart is good medicine" (Prov. 17:22). We all need to laugh more. If exercise puts us in a better frame of mind to do that, then we should all be exercising.

How Important Is Exercise to Me Really?

By exercising you will reap the benefits of a stronger heart, more powerful lungs, and better- toned muscles. Plus you'll increase your metabolism and likely shed a few pounds. Hallelujah! That's what I want; maybe you do too.

In addition, you'll be a great example to your family, and you'll be teaching them something that may save their lives. Turn off that TV, grab those little hands, and take your family for a walk. Let's get moving and change our families.

I've heard every excuse because I've used them all: "I'm too tired." "I can't afford it." "Who will stay with the kids?" "It's too cold." "It's too hot." "I don't like to sweat." "I tried it, and it doesn't work." Listen, no more excuses. Many of us have access to group exercise programs, gyms, aerobics, Pilates, yoga, community pools, walking trails, even dancing classes. Most communities have made exercise easy for us.

THE TREADMILL—
WHERE PERSISTENCE IS REWARDED

Let me tell you: I love those senior rates at the gym, and taking a brisk thirty-minute walk is exhilarating.

Decide What's Best for You and Get Moving!

Endurance exercises not only increase your breathing and heart rate but also improve the health of your heart, lungs, and circulatory system. More endurance keeps you healthier and improves your stamina; it may delay or even prevent many diseases such as diabetes, colon cancer, heart disease, stroke, and so on.

Strength exercises build your muscles, increase your metabolism, and help keep your weight and blood sugar in check. They may also help prevent osteoporosis.

Examples of Endurance Activities

Moderate

Swimming
Bicycling
Cycling on a stationary bicycle
Gardening, mowing, raking
Walking briskly on a level surface
Mopping or scrubbing floors
Golf without a cart
Tennis (doubles)
Volleyball
Rowing
Dancing

Vigorous

Climbing stairs or hills
Shoveling snow

Brisk bicycling up hills
Tennis (singles)
Swimming laps
Cross-country skiing
Downhill skiing
Hiking
Jogging

Tip: Here's a simple idea to put exercise and volunteering together. Next time you go for a walk, take a plastic bag and pick up trash. You're going to keep your little corner of the world beautiful and perhaps even inspire someone else to do the same.

Keeping It Simple

Finally, there's no denying that exercise is one key to a healthier, happier lifestyle. I once thought that exercise had to be a major activity like going to the gym six days a week or running a marathon (by the way, I'm so happy for those who are able to do these activities). But you and I can work exercise into our daily routines by walking after dinner or taking the stairs instead of the elevator. A moderately paced walking program is the simplest thing we can do. Riding a bike, dancing, or playing tennis are all good activities too. Exercise is the single best thing we can do for ourselves. Actually, any kind of physical activity can lift our spirits. Even mopping a floor for twenty minutes can be a mood changer. Daily activities will knock down distress and depression every time.

For those who are looking for a plan, at the end of this chapter I've included six strength exercises you can easily do in your own home with just a chair, athletic shoes, and a pair of hand weights. For more information about health and

THE TREADMILL—
WHERE PERSISTENCE IS REWARDED

exercise, go to the National Institute for Health's Web site at http://www.nih.gov. Most importantly, be sure to consult your doctor or health care professional before you begin any exercise program, especially if you have experienced back, knee, elbow or shoulder pain.

Shaping Your Body with Six Simple Exercises

Yes, you can do it! You *can* reshape your body. Strength training using hand weights or even your own body weight will help build and sculpt muscles whether you're eighteen or eighty. One eighty-two-year-old woman who began these exercises told me that it wasn't long before she had more energy during the day and was sleeping better at night.

Here Are a Few Tips

- A complete move is called a "lift" or "repetition." A lift takes about nine seconds—four to lift the weight, one to pause, and four to return the weight to the starting position.
- Stretch before and after your routine to prevent injury and increase flexibility.
- Concentrate on good posture to avoid muscle strain or injury.
- Do lifts slowly. You won't train your muscles if momentum or gravity does the work. To avoid holding your breath, a common mistake, count out loud while you're doing your routine.
- Don't begin with weights that are too heavy. You should be able to complete each lift eight times while maintaining good form. Be sure to rest afterward. Increase the weight when the eighth lift is no longer a challenge.

- Avoid pain. This is a signal that you are pushing yourself too hard.
- Allow yourself a day or two off between sessions to give your muscles a chance to rest.
- Keep a log of your progress. Record weight lifted and the number of lifts and sets performed. One set equals eight lifts. Noting your progress is great motivation.

Reasons Why

With strength training, you not only lose weight but also give yourself a leaner, healthier body of someone who is naturally slim. Strength training also helps to prevent muscle and bone loss in an especially vulnerable group— women, regardless of age, who are dieting.

Many women are shocked to learn that women who diet are an at-risk category. Many of us have thought that when we lose weight, our bodies burn only excess fat. Researchers have discovered that when women diet without exercise, between 20 and 25 percent of the weight they shed is water, muscle, bone, and other lean tissue. The less muscle you have, the harder it is to lose weight and maintain its loss. The reason? Muscle is metabolically active, whereas body fat is inactive.

With this plan we're not talking "Ms. Olympia" with heavy weights, lengthy workouts, and steroids. This plan requires only three twenty-minute sessions per week.

Getting Started

During the first week, most women work with one-pound weights (a narrow one-pound can of corn is fine for starters) so they can concentrate on form. Because you'll move quickly up the weight scale, I suggest that you purchase pairs of dumbbells (three pounds, five pounds, six pounds, eight pounds, and ten pounds) as you move along.

Other than a sturdy chair and athletic shoes, that's all you'll need! You won't need to join a gym or buy expensive equipment. You can exercise right there in your own home or office.

The Program

1. Chair Stand, Version 1. Sit on edge of chair and cross arms over chest. Keep your back straight. Lean forward slightly and stand. Pause and return to seated position. When you can easily complete two sets, advance to Version 2.

2. Chair Stand, Version 2. Stand in front of chair, turning your toes out slightly. Extend arms straight out in front of you. Keep your back straight and your knees positioned above your ankles. While continuing to extend arms, bend at hips and lower yourself into

sitting position in chair. Pause, then stand back up to starting position. You may add intensity by lowering yourself almost to seated position and hovering. Pause and then rise again.

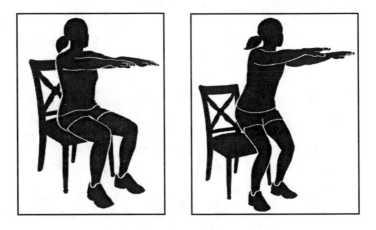

3. Overhead Press. While standing, hold a dumbbell in each hand at shoulder level, parallel to floor, palms forward. (If you experience shoulder problems, turn palms and weights to face each other.) Extend arms over head, then lower to original position.

4. Bent-Over Row. Sit forward in chair. Let arms hang down at sides, palms facing in, with a dumbbell in each hand. Tighten abdominal muscles for stability. Bend slightly forward at the waist with your back straight. While elbows are bent and wrists straight, pull both dumbbells straight up as high as you are able. Pause and then lower to starting position.

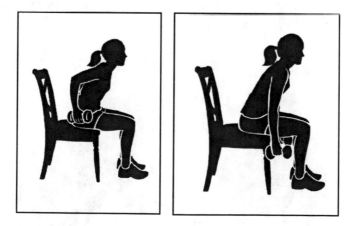

5. Calf Raise. Stand with fingertips resting lightly on the back of a sturdy chair. Rise up on the balls of your

feet as high as you are able. Hold for three seconds and then lower heels to original position.

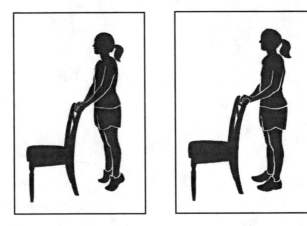

6. Seated Fly. Sit forward in chair. With upper arms against sides, hold a dumbbell in each hand, palms facing thighs. With elbows slightly bent, lift upper arms straight out to shoulder height. At the end of lift, upper arms and forearms should be parallel to floor. Pause and then lower arms.

 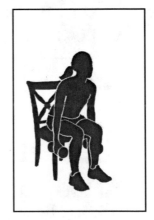

7. Arm Curl. Stand with arms down at sides while holding dumbbells, palms facing thighs. Keep elbows pressed gently against sides. Rotate and raise only forearms, palms now facing up. Move dumbbells up to front of shoulders in one smooth motion. Pause, then lower arms, rotating forearms to starting position.

Can these exercises make a difference? You bet. Though these are small steps at first, this program will take you as far as you want to go.

The Treadmill—Where Persistence Is Rewarded

Get ready! Reflect: What do my habits—good and bad—look like?

How are they working for me?

Get set! Pray and plan: Is there something I should change?

Go! Take action: What's the first step? When will I begin?

To get the most out of your fitness routine, Dr. Robert Sallis, a family and sports medicine physician at Kaiser Permanente suggests the F.I.T.T. principle:[11]

Frequency: Exercise most days of the week, at least five days.

Intensity: Exercise at a rate that allows you to talk while exercising.

Time: Exercise thirty to fifty minutes per session.

Type: Choose an activity like jogging, swimming, walking, or dancing that works major muscle groups and gets your heart rate up.

Prayer

Dear Lord, I have learned things that I know are important. Would you help me to incorporate an exercise routine into my life that will help me look and feel better, thus making me the best ever for my family? I want to keep my family secure in this shaky world. In Jesus' name, amen.

CHAPTER 6

. . . .

THE PRAYER
CLOSET—
WHERE FAITH IS
STRENGTHENED

"He hears the prayer of the righteous."
—Proverbs 15:29

D ID YOU KNOW that church services about prayer
are often the least attended events? Why is that?
We know we should pray. We tell ourselves we
will. We make commitments and buy books to read and
journals to write in, but when it comes right down to it, we
miss the mark. In the next few pages, I hope to encourage
and excite you about your prayer life. Prayer is one of the
most important things we can do for ourselves and those
we love.

Definition of Prayer

When you read the Psalms, you will see that King David
lived his life in prayer. Many of them bring tears to my
eyes, for I often see myself in them. Look closely. You will
see yourself there too. Prayers were on David's mind, his

heart, and his lips. He wasn't afraid to bare his soul before the Lord, acknowledge his need, and ask for help. David prayed as Paul tells us to in 1 Thessalonians 5:17: "pray without ceasing." David knew from experience that God would hear his prayer and "give ear to the words of [his] mouth" (Ps. 54:2). Oswald Chambers, one of my favorite devotional writers, said,

> It is not part of the life of a natural man to pray. What will suffer is the life of the Son of God in him, which is nourished not by food, but by prayer. When a man is born from above, the life of the Son of God is born in him, and he can either starve that life or nourish it. Prayer is the way the life of God is nourished. We look upon prayer as a means of getting things for ourselves; the *Bible's idea of prayer is that we may get to know God Himself* [emphasis added].

Wow, I needed that.

Hindrances

How do we pray when we're as busy as we are—and getting busier? Our generation of women have more on their plates than at any other time, though the pioneer women were busy from sunup to sundown. We've been told that today we have life so much easier with our washing machines, driers, dishwashers, Crock-Pots, microwaves, computers, cell phones, and a dozen other things that supposedly make our lives better. But those conveniences have enabled us to pile so much into our lives that we don't have a moment in our day without a commitment tied to it. Lord, save us from these conveniences that "help" us.

In addition, we have an enemy who wants to keep us from prayer. Jonathan Edwards said, "The one concern of the devil is to keep the saints from prayer. He fears nothing from prayerless studies, prayerless work and prayerless religion. He laughs at our toil, mocks at our wisdom, but he trembles when we pray."

"What's the devil's strategy?" you ask. That's to keep you tired, busy, and frustrated. Sometimes the last thing we feel like doing or think we have time for is prayer, but that's what we need to do the most.

Why Pray? Scripture Commands It

Jesus is always our example. In the New Testament we frequently see that He got up early to pray in a quiet place (Mark 1:35; Luke 5:16; 6:12). In Matthew 26:41, one of Jesus' last instructions to His disciples was to "keep watching and praying."

Why Pray? Prayer Is Good for You

If we could sit together and talk, I bet you could give testimony today of trials and burdens you've laid at the foot of the cross. Great peace fills us when we pour our souls out to God. We look better and feel better. I think we even live longer, and what an example we are to others! You can be sure that when we pray and experience God's peace, people are going to ask us what our secret is. Then we'll have the opportunity of a lifetime to tell them all about it.

Why Pray? Prayer Changes Things and People

I had a praying grandmother. When I was born, my parents wanted nothing to do with church. My grandmother was the only Christian who knew me, and I discovered many years later that she had faithfully prayed for me.

Maybe you have a grandmother or mother like that, or maybe you're a grandmother who is praying for your grandchildren. May I encourage you not to falter. Keep it up. My grandmother's prayers were answered in big ways, and we'll talk more about that a little later.

Why Pray? Prayer Helps You Get to Know God Better

God is good and kind. He's gracious and compassionate. He's slow to anger, and He abounds in lovingkindness. He wants to bless us, and when we *really* know Him, we will find that we want to please Him more. It's the real circle of life that never ends. He gives us Himself. We give. He gives. We give. He gives, and on it goes. God reveals Himself more and more as we get to know Him through our prayers.

Many years ago, I was out walking and praying. I had prayed about something. I don't remember the exact details of now, but what I do remember is that God had miraculously answered a prayer that only He and I knew about.

It finally hit me. I stopped dead in my tracks and said aloud, "Wow! You really do love me, don't You?" The Scripture popped into my mind. "We love, because He first loved us" (1 John 4:19). When you talk to God about all the little nitty-gritty details and see Him involved in your life, you will learn to love Him more and more. You see, He cares for you and longs to show you how much.

Why Pray? Your Prayer Life Is an Example to Others

Whether you're a mom, a grandmother, a sister, an aunt, or a daughter, it doesn't matter; you will be the glue that holds your family together. You may be the only stable influence it has. When you are praying, it makes a difference.

My children have told me that they take great comfort in knowing that I am praying for them regularly.

Dr. David Jeremiah says, "Whenever prayer becomes a priority, it sets in motion the power of God." Do you know that you have access to the hearts of your husband and children and loved ones through the power of prayer? (See Prov. 21:1.) If we're not praying for those close to us, who will? We're the ones who love them the most.

Every great spiritual awakening in a heart or in a place has begun with prayer. When we intercede for our husband's job, for a granddaughter in trouble, for a mother having surgery, for a neighbor who needs Christ, for a teen in rehab, or for a pastor who needs strength, we are asking God to provide for that person something we can't provide. We are acting as go-betweens, asking God to direct His power in a specific direction. More than that, when we see God answer in some way and involve Himself in our lives and in our prayers, our faith increases as never before.

Simply put, prayer helps us to recognize our needs. Prayer teaches us to care, and prayer brings God's presence into our lives. That's what I want. How about you?

Summer and Blue Eyes

One summer our whole family worked at Indian Hills Bible Camp, located in the beautiful hills of Jamul, California, not far from San Diego. The following is a true story of what happened one day:

> "Mom, look! Aren't they adorable? Can we pleeease keep them? You won't have to do anything. I'll take care of 'em. I promise."

> On no! Thirteen-year-old Jennifer had two white, blue-eyed kittens in her arms. We didn't have the time or the

money for pets. I struggled just getting the laundry done and keeping things organized in our household of eight. She said she'd take care of them, but I knew these kittens would grow up to be not-so-cute-anymore cats. And guess who would be taking care of them then? Looking into Jennifer's wide, expectant eyes, I didn't have the heart to say no. "OK, we'll try it, but they have to stay in the garage. No exceptions. And the first time you neglect them, they're history."

"Thanks, Mom. You're the greatest." She gave me a hug and ran off yelling to her sisters and brother, "Look what I have. Mom said we can keep them."

Jennifer named her kittens Summer and Blue Eyes and they were the hit of the family. Amy and Sarah had them attend tea parties and took them on more than one walk in a doll stroller, dressed in baby clothes. They didn't seem to mind, and I had to admit Jennifer was following through on her end of the deal.

It wasn't long, however, before we had other problems. Three-year-old Amy began wheezing. We discovered that she is severely allergic to cats. Day after day I warned her, "Amy, don't touch those cats…Amy, wash your hands." This was an impossible task for a little girl who loved animals. Her wheezing got worse. The cats had to go.

We offered them to friends and put signs around the neighborhood, at the supermarket, and in the children's schools. No takers. We didn't want to think about the animal shelter, knowing what their fate would be, but it seemed our only option.

I couldn't do it, so my husband took Summer and Blue Eyes on that grim ride to the shelter. He returned more despondent than I'd ever seen him, stating, "Don't ask me to ever do that again." We all sat down to dinner in total silence.

"OK, guys, we're going to pray." Immediately all heads bowed. We held tightly to each other's hands, Jennifer brushed tears from her cheek and I prayed, "Lord, please take care of Summer and Blue Eyes. They're probably frightened. Find someone who loves little blue-eyed kittens and who will take good care of them. Amen."

Three days later I opened our local newspaper, and two white, blue-eyed kittens stared back at me from the front page. Summer and Blue Eyes! The caption said they had just been brought to the animal shelter and needed a good home. They were going to be on an adopt-a-pet van at our shopping mall the upcoming weekend.

"Jennifer, Sarah, Amy, look at this!" When they saw the picture, their expressions were priceless. "You know, I've heard good things about this adopt-a-pet program. They always find homes for the animals. Someone is going to fall in love with our kittens and take them home."[12]

I want my kids to see that God operates not only in the lives of missionaries and Bible characters but also in our lives. This was a teachable moment, and I will cherish it for as long as I live. Nothing I could tell my children would illustrate more beautifully the fact that God cares about each of them and the little details of their lives, including a home for two little kittens. It began with a prayer and ended with a wonderful conclusion. He wants to show all of us how much He cares, and sometimes He even puts it in the newspaper.

My Cousin and the Astronaut

One morning I was listening to a popular Christian radio program in which Charlie Duke was being interviewed. I knew that Charlie Duke was a well-known astronaut, but I didn't know he was a dedicated Christian. I listened intently as he described his flights and how magnificent God's creation in outer space was from his viewpoint. He said that he lived in a small Texas town, and I realized to my surprise that my cousin Joan and her husband, John, live in the same town!

I began to pray, and my prayer went something like this: "Lord, I don't believe in coincidences. Charlie Duke is a Christian, and he lives in the same town where my cousin does. Charlie Duke is a wonderful spokesperson for You, Lord. I would love for Joan and John to meet him. Could You, would You, get them together sometime? Lord, I thank You and praise You. Amen."

My cousin's husband, John, owns an elite flight training school. People from all walks of life come in to fly and train. The next time I called John, he told me, "Hey Judy, guess who came into the center today? Charlie Duke. You know, the famous astronaut. Boy, he's a nice guy. You and he talk about the same kinds of things. I'll bet you would really like him. He invited us to go to church with him, and we just might do that one of these days."

You never know what seeds are planted or how God will use them, but the key is this: keep praying!

Keeping a Record

One day I was thinking about some of my prayers and how God had answered them. Time had gone by, and I'd forgotten some of the details. I realized then and there that I needed to get them down on paper, or they would be lost.

I pulled out an empty notebook, decorated the front and back cover with pictures of my kids and grandkids, and made sections inside for each family member. I began writing down all my prayers and the answers I could remember. I call it my "leaving a legacy notebook." I write in pencil, pen, marker—whatever's available. It's not the prettiest journal, but that's not the point. I want to look through this book with my family and tell them, "Look what God did here and here and here."

Actually, God invented the idea of visual aids. In the book of Joshua, Chapter 4, He told the Israelites to erect stones. Each time they looked at them, it reminded them to tell their children the great things the Lord had done. Our prayer journals will be our pile of stones.

Did you know that it takes only the negligence of one generation for God's goodness to be forgotten? We need remembrances lest we forget. You may be journaling and making a notebook already. If so, I say, "Good for you. Keep up the good work." Get those blessings down so you can leave a legacy for your family.

Christmas Cards in a Basket

Every year I take all the Christmas cards mailed to our home and place them in a basket on our dining room table. Each morning after my husband and I read Scripture, we pray for someone who sent us a Christmas card. Then I send a personal note to that person or family, letting them know that we prayed for them that morning and listing a few specific things we prayed for. At least one-third of the cards we receive come from families who do not know Jesus.

One year we bought a gas log fireplace from a local business. Of course, the business wanted to increase sales, so personnel sent us a Christmas card. One morning in

January we selected their Christmas card from the basket and prayed for those working there. This is what I wrote in the personal note to them:

To the staff at _____Fireside Shop,

You won't remember us. We were customers last year. My husband and I pray for those whom we received Christmas cards from and your card came up today. Aren't you glad you sent one to us?

We don't know you by name and I can only visualize one or two faces, but the Lord knows your names, your faces and even the numbers of hairs on your head. Literally everything about you. And better yet, He loves each one of you with an everlasting love and He has a wonderful plan for your lives. We prayed that each one of you would experience the love He has for you and that you would come to know Him personally.

This morning we thanked Him for your friendliness and integrity that you showed us when we shopped at your store. We love our gas log arrangement. We hope He blesses you *with much success as you continue to do business.*

Very Sincerely,
Richard and Judy Scharfenberg

I have no idea what those employees thought when they read this letter. It probably made the rounds, and I'm sure there was some laughter. That's OK. I know God will use the message in their lives sometime somewhere. He has promised, "So shall My word be which goes forth from My mouth; It shall not return to Me empty, without accomplishing what I desire, and without succeeding in the matter for which I sent it" (Isa. 55:11).

Do you have unsaved family members? Do you know people in your neighborhood or at work who don't know the Lord? Do you sometimes face tough situations and feel helpless? Did you know that God turns hearts like channels of water? Get creative. Sit down, kneel down, fall down, and pray. Prayer is one thing you will never regret.

The Prayer Closet—Where Faith Is Strengthened

Get ready! Reflect: What do my habits—good and bad—look like?

How are they working for me?

Get set! Pray and plan: Is there something I should change?

Go! Take action: What's the first step? When will I begin?

Sadly, time for prayer is at the end of our lists. We don't do it on purpose, but when we are asked about our prayer lives, all of us would agree that prayer is important. When an athlete trains consistently, his actions become automatic. Christians should discipline themselves to develop spiritual reflexes. Do you know what that means? It means we should "pray without ceasing" (1 Thess. 5:17).

Prayer

"Yes, Father, I confess that my prayer life is lacking. May this be a turning point. I want to regularly add prayer to my schedule, and may I begin today. These are perhaps just baby steps, but that's OK. Give me a plan and help me to be faithful to do it. In Jesus' name, amen."

CHAPTER 7

THE QUIET TIME—
WHERE GOD IS
ENCOUNTERED

"....The tent of the upright will flourish."
—Proverbs 14:11

JESUS, THE AUTHOR of joy, says in Mark 6:31, "Come away by yourselves to a lonely place and rest awhile." And we answer, "My day is full. I have a million things to do, and I'm already exhausted. How will I do that?"

A day in the life of a friend:

I poke a hand out of my covers and silence the alarm. Retracting my arm to my side, I lie still, eyes closed, deciding if I have the will to get up.

The night before, I set my alarm so I could get to work early. Somehow, an eight-to-five workday is never enough time to reduce the pile waiting for me on my desk. I force myself out of bed and head for the shower.

Forty minutes later I make a last-minute run through the house, checking the iron, shutting off lights. I manage to lock the front door while balancing a cup of coffee and grabbing an energy bar, my purse, bills to be mailed, a gym bag, and my briefcase. Then I hop in my car and race down the road, leaving behind a quiet house and a Bible sitting unnoticed on the nightstand.

Tomorrow, I will probably do it all over again.

Sound familiar? This dear woman tells the story of thousands just like her.

I did the math. Did you know that after fifteen years, a mother of three has probably washed at least 5,475 loads of laundry, prepared 10,950 meals, packed 12,105 lunches, and wiped noses at least 14,600 times. If her children had allergies, you can increase that number. She's gotten up 1,095 nights with a sick or fussy baby and changed 17,520 diapers.

It's hard to find a quiet time, yet Jesus still beckons, "Come away and rest awhile" (Mark 6:31).

We all experience frustration when our time is not our own. I've been there. I remember days when four of my children were eight and under. Finding time alone isn't easy when you've been up all night, the laundry is piling up, two active preschoolers need your attention, your hungry husband is about to walk through the door any minute, and you haven't even thought about what to prepare for dinner, let alone start it. Or maybe you just don't feel like reading your Bible.

Remember Karen whom I was counseling? I asked her at one of our sessions how much time she was spending in devotions or a quiet time. You remember that she was too tired to exercise and it was the same for her quiet time. She told me she didn't feel up to reading her Bible or praying and I hadn't seen her in church for a long time.

You know, God doesn't leave us; we leave Him, but even on our worst days, we have a lot to thank Him for:

- His promise never to leave us
- The home we live in and the food on the table
- Our family and friends
- The privilege of worshipping regularly
- Our home in heaven
- (You fill in the blank.) _____
- (You fill in the blank.) _____

Faithfulness Is the Key

Regular, consistent time with the Lord will not happen automatically. We must work at it. Remember, we have an enemy who is out to get us. Satan will contest every moment you spend in Bible reading or prayer. It never ceases to amaze me how many rabbit trails I can follow on the way to my quiet time. Being committed is a battle, and we must plan, prepare, concentrate, and focus.

It's very important to memorize Scripture and sing hymns and praise songs regularly. These are ways to keep our minds focused, but we need material to draw from. What you put in your mind stays there and will come up at the oddest moments. After a Sunday service, I find myself humming and singing the songs I sang in church for days afterward. God tells us in Colossians 3:16 to "let the word of Christ richly dwell within you, with all wisdom teaching and admonishing one another with psalms and hymns and spiritual songs, singing with thankfulness in your hearts to God." I love it when this happens.

Make a Plan

Singing in your heart is a great way to spend the day, but we need a definite quiet time with the Lord as well. Some of you will discover that early morning is most convenient; others will prefer late at night, and still others may spend time during the day. Whenever it is, your quiet time should be a fixed time. It's pretty sad when we make sure we eat meals and have time for recreation and sleep but leave the needs of our souls to take care of themselves. Cultivate a sense of need, and that will soon help you to be creative. Quiet time with the Lord should be fixed and as much a part of our day as a shower and a meal.

Find a quiet place. This is where the creative part comes in. I know about large families in small homes where every space is filled with something. It may be difficult for you to get alone. The challenge is easier for me now that my adult children are married and out of our home.

At this time in my life I head to a corner in my living room, where I open the blinds and let the early dawn break through. I always use a basket, where I put my Bible, journal, (I buy several inexpensive spiral notebooks when school supplies go on sale.) pens, pencils, index cards, the current Bible study I am working on, a book of praise songs and hymns, and any other aid I'm currently using to make my quiet time more meaningful. I remember the days when I kept this basket high on a shelf, away from small hands. I would pull it down and sit at the kitchen table before the family got up. During the summer I sometimes go out on the patio. I love being out in the fresh new morning looking at God's beautiful creation.

I always take time for devotions in the morning. That's the quiet time at my house, and it's when I find I have the most energy. I begin with singing. I go through an old hymnal and a book of praise songs, singing a song or two each morning. I read Scripture from a read-through-the-Bible-in-a-year guide, pray, and then write in my journal. I try to spend at least forty-five minutes, but many times my quiet time is longer because I find myself interested and involved.

Once in a while I miss a day, but this is going to happen. I try to be as consistent in my quiet time as possible because I've found that when I miss it, I'm a different person. I *need* to spend time with Jesus. I *need* to get to know Him better. I *need* to praise Him and show my love. I always come away from my devotional time with my heart softer and a pleasant look on my face. In no way can any of us spend quality time with the Lord, time spent loving and praising Him, and not be changed.

Like me you probably struggle and wonder, *What Bible study should I do?* Hundreds of studies are available. I wish I had the money I've spent on books I've never read and studies I've never done. Like I've said so many times, "I don't have this gray hair for nothing." Let me share with you some ideas that have worked for me.

First, it's a good practice to read the Bible through each year. You may be doing that already, but if not, you'll find many free reading plans online; simply find the one that works best for you and get started. Your local Christian bookstore may have inexpensive plans available in booklet form. I've been reading the Bible through for many years and still find it fresh and new. I can't tell you how many times I've said to my husband, "I never saw that verse before." It never grows old.

If you read every day and listen with your eyes on the pages of your Bible, God will speak to you. Let me give you an example. Here's an entry from one of my journal pages.

September 15—Lord, You never cease to amaze me. I
was impatient with Richard this morning. He seemed so
unreasonable. I tried to show him my side, but naturally
the conflict got worse, totally blown out of proportion.
I know if I'd been kinder to begin with, it might never
have happened, but I was so stubborn. Now he's really
bent and won't go to therapy (because of his stroke
in 1998) no matter how much I backtrack and try to
apologize.

I don't want to, but I sit down to do my devotions
and what's scheduled for me to read today? First
Corinthians 13—Love never fails. Great. I read it,
grudgingly at first, but it finally penetrates, and I have
to ask myself, "Am I truly loving Richard the way Christ
wants me to? Do I suffer long and am I kind? Do I
envy and parade myself around? Am I puffed up; do I
behave rudely and only see my own way? Do I rejoice
in iniquity or the truth? Do I bear all things, believe
all things, hope all things, endure all things? Because,
Judy, love never fails."

Whew! Thank You, Lord, for catching me and revealing
my ugly, selfish nature.

> O Love that will not let me go,
> I rest my weary soul in thee;
> I give thee back the life I owe,
> That in thine ocean depths its flow
> May richer, fuller be.[13]

I want what You want, Lord. Here I am. Use me again.

When will we learn that life is not about us but about
Him? When we practice His presence, giving Him our time,
He will speak to us.

What Bible Study Should I Do?

We've talked about the myriad of Bible studies available. Ask your church's women's ministries director, go online, check your local Christian bookstores, or ask your friends. Just do your homework and find the best one for you. In the meantime, here are three studies that require only you, your Bible, and writing material.

- Read Paul's letters: Romans, 1 and 2 Corinthians, Galatians, Ephesians, Philippians, Colossians, 1 and 2 Thessalonians, 1 and 2 Timothy, Titus and Philemon in the New Testament. This is a lot of reading, but don't let it overwhelm you. Just take your time. As you read, write down everything Paul prayed about. You might want to read a biography of Paul. I absolutely loved *Paul, A Man of Grace and Grit*, by Charles R. Swindoll, and you can probably find this at the library. What an eye-opener! When you read about Paul's life and the horrific conditions he experienced and then read his prayers, his letters will make you weep.
- Read Isaiah 40-66 three separate times. The first time through, write down everything you can about the nature and character of God. During the second time through, write down the nature and character of man. During the third time through, write down God's commitment to man. God's graciousness in dealing with us will stagger you. You'll love Him even more.

The following is a worksheet you can copy to use for a study. Read any Scripture of your choosing and then answer the following questions in your notebook:

- Read—As you read, underline anything that stands out as something that will help you.
- Write—List important facts. What does the text say?
- Understand—Are there lessons to be learned? What does the text mean?
- Personalize—How does the text affect you? List the lessons you learned and form them as a question. For example, remember my journal entry about when I was upset with my husband? I had to admit that I was only thinking of myself and that was sin. And then I had to ask myself, do I truly love Richard the way Christ wants me to? Do I suffer long and am I kind? Do I envy and parade myself around?
- Pray—What have you learned? Is God speaking to you? Ask Him to help you apply these lessons to your life.

King David penned these words in Psalm 27:13-14, "I would have despaired unless I had believed that I would see the goodness of the Lord in the land of the living. Wait for the Lord; be strong and let your heart take courage; yes, wait for the Lord."

Words Worth Considering

"Let any man turn to God in earnest, let him begin to exercise himself unto godliness, let him seek to develop his powers of spiritual receptivity by trust and obedience and humility, and the results will exceed anything he may have hoped in his leaner and weaker days."
—A.W. Tozer

More Bible Reading Tips

1. Start today. You will find no better time, and you have no reason to wait.

2. Choose a specific time each day. Set your schedule and then stick to it. Mornings are great, but your schedule may not permit that. Find the time that works consistently for you.

3. Read for the sake of learning, not simply to get through your next reading. Always start with a short prayer before you begin. Ask God to keep you focused, give you wisdom and understanding, and then be refreshed, changed, and strengthened by the words you read!

The Quiet Time—Where God Is Encountered

Get ready! Reflect: What do my habits—good and bad— look like?

How are they working for me?

Get set! Pray and plan: Is there something I should change?

Go! Take action: What's the first step? When will I begin?

The Lord says to you and me, "I'll help you get connected. I'll build your character. I'll help you to discover joy. I'll test your faith and reward your persistence. I'll show you how to encounter more of Me. Choose a plan and let's get started."

Prayer

Lord, would you open my eyes so I can clearly see and understand Your Word? I want to obey it with all of my heart. Guide me and teach me. May I eagerly listen to You and follow You all the days of my life. In Jesus' name, amen.

. . . .

CHAPTER 8

THE PERFECT
FAMILY

W HEN I WAS a girl there was a very popular TV
program called *Father Knows Best*. I watched
it every week without fail. I can still see Jim
Anderson, who was father, played by Robert Young, walk
through the door and announce, "Margaret, I'm home!" And
that Margaret! She'd waltz to the door in a dress and high
heels, her hair and makeup just perfect. Can you imagine?
I don't know about you, but when I'm comfortable at home
I'm wearing jeans and no makeup.

That program was the picture of a perfect family to
me.

My Perfect Family

For the first few years of my life, in my little girl mind
I was part of the perfect family. I lived in Ohio with my
mom, dad, and younger brother. I was surrounded by
grandparents, aunts and uncles, and dozens of cousins.
Another set of grandparents lived on a farm in Indiana. I

loved that farm. I wish every child could visit a farm like that.

When the Japanese bombed Pearl Harbor on December 7, 1941, my dad joined the navy. My mom, brother, and I stayed in Ohio while he went to war. When I was ten, he received orders to go to San Diego, California. Suddenly, we were moving. Oh, the excitement was almost unbearable! California seemed like the end of the world, but I had heard good things about life there, and I could hardly wait. We spent three long days and nights on a train that snaked across the country, but finally we arrived.

Dad rented a ramshackle house that looked like it was built on stilts. It had a long pier that inched out into the water and overlooked Mission Bay. The house had been the old Mission Bay Yacht Club, but when the owner could no longer use it for large crowds, he rented it out for single family use. The house was quite primitive and hard to keep clean, but my brother Dave and I let Mom worry about that. We loved it.

We lived on the beach, a literal paradise where I learned to swim. Dave and I walked on the beach, built sandcastles, found unusual creatures stranded on the beach, and baked in the sun. This was long before we knew how damaging the sun was. We enjoyed the blue skies and balmy breezes, and eagerly looked forward to making friends at school.

This should have been the place in the story when they all lived happily ever after. But it wasn't long before my perfect family began to fall apart.

Falling Apart

The drinking began, and terrible fights broke out every weekend. Things went from bad to worse. It was horrible, and Dave and I were scared. This problem didn't develop overnight. It had been building up for a long time; I just hadn't noticed it. But then I saw things no little girl should see.

When I was thirteen, not a good age for kids in even the best circumstances, my parents divorced. I watched my dad walk away and wondered, *What are we going to do?* Mom had always stayed home with Dave and me; she was young and had never worked outside the home. I knew she couldn't take care of us.

You guessed it. We lived through some pretty rough years.

Surviving

I heard Dr. Phil say on one of his television programs[14] that when he was growing up, his family was so poor that they ate catsup sandwiches. I knew just what he was talking about. Many times we didn't have any food in the house. We didn't have any money either.

My brother was once a pinsetter at our local bowling alley. Mom and I always knew he'd come home with a few tips. One day Dave walked in the door with a big smile stretching from ear to ear and lots of coins jingling in his pocket. He and I raced to Harry's Market to buy bread, mayonnaise, bologna, and cheese. Then we ran home as fast as we could. We slapped those sandwiches together and crammed them down faster than you could blink.

With my cheeks stuffed like a chipmunk, I told Mom, "This is the best sandwich I've ever had." Even to this day I love bologna and cheese, but I don't eat them anymore. For some compelling reason, I always wolf them down—and it's not pretty.

I suppose if it were today, we might have been homeless, but somehow we got by. Children are resilient and usually find ways to adjust, but Mom's way of coping was to drink from morning till night. Today my heart aches when I think about her responsibilities and how overwhelming life must have been for her, but my reaction then was embarrassment and anger. I'm ashamed when I say this, but I often ridiculed her, saying horrible things. I hated what alcohol did to her.

Mornings were a whole different story. I loved them. She was sober and did what all Moms do. Fixing our breakfast, packing lunches and sending us off with a smile made me hopeful that it would stay that way, but when we came home from school, she wasn't the same woman. Dave and I were left on our own most of the time. You know, it's scary for a kid to be in charge of their own world.

Memories and Longings

Now you can imagine why *Father Knows Best* appealed to me. I watched that program with longing in my heart. I wanted my family to be like the family on that show. I wanted to sit at their table with Jim Anderson as my dad. I wanted my mom to be like Margaret. The program reminded me of the happy times before my parents' divorce when we visited my grandparents' farm.

That was where our whole family ate meals together at a dining room table laden with food on Franciscan Ware Desert Rose dishes. We said grace, nobody cursed, and there were no arguments. We went to church on Sundays and sang the old hymns. I loved it at grandma's and never wanted to leave. To this day the sight of a two-story farmhouse with attic bedrooms and quilts on the bed makes me cry every time.

Because I had especially loved the secure feeling when I went to church with my grandma back in Ohio, I tried to recapture that sensation by attending a church just a mile from my house in California. I liked the way I felt during those few hours on Sunday morning—safe and secure with families and grandmas surrounding me. I remember thinking, *I'll pretend this is my perfect family.*

Church attendance lasted for a few years, but it wasn't long before I was a teenager. None of my friends were going to church. "Church is for squares," they said. So I quit going.

Too Young to Be on My Own

Somehow I made it through the tenth grade. But with no supervision, I dated far too young, became pregnant, and was married at the age of seventeen. I can't believe it when I say it. I was just a baby myself. My young husband was no more ready for marriage than I was. Neither of us knew that a good marriage took working together and looking out for the needs of the other person. We didn't know that marriage was sacrifice, and selflessness. The only thing either of us was interested in was our own happiness and well-being.

The marriage was destined for failure. We had a son. I named him David after my brother, and when I was pregnant with our daughter, Melissa, we separated and divorced. On the day I came home from the hospital with my new baby girl, I wondered how I would take care of these two little ones. I was twenty years old and scared to death.

Fortunately, I found a job at Pacific Telephone Company. It was a good job, but I was overwhelmed by working full time, figuring out childcare, finding someone to care for my kids when they were sick and I still had to go work, making sure mechanics didn't rip me off when my car needed repairs, and managing a household. I was frightened and discouraged, but the years passed by. Again, somehow we got by.

Once in a while after the kids were in bed I watched a romantic movie and dreamed about being rescued by a knight in shining armor—you know, like in the fairy tales. But then I told myself, "Grow up, Judy. It's not gonna happen. This is real life."

Some Fairy Tales Come True

I used to shop at a little store near my house on the way home from work. Believe me, I noticed Richard, the handsome clerk; in fact, that's one of the reasons I stopped by. He was always friendly, but on one particular night he said, "Your daughter was in today to buy an ice cream."

This was a neighborhood store, and it was safe then for children to walk to the store for ice cream. David and Melissa did it all the time. The practice wasn't unusual, so I wondered why he had mentioned it. I gave him a puzzled look.

Then he said, "She told me you're divorced."

That little squirt. My heart began pounding. I looked up at him. "Why, yes, I am."

"May I call you sometime?"

I looked into his gorgeous blue eyes and was so nervous I didn't think I could talk, but somehow I managed, "Yes, that would be nice."

Perhaps I appeared cool and collected, but my insides were shaking like Jell-O®. I left the store wanting to kick my heels in the air. But as hard as it was, I controlled myself and slowly sauntered to my car.

You would have been really proud of me. It was only when I was halfway down the street that I let out a squeal I'll bet even Richard could have heard. Not once in a million years did I ever think a nice man like Richard would be interested in me.

The next week seemed like a year as I waited for his call. Finally, he did call, and we began dating, and he was everything I had ever dreamed of. He endeared himself to me from the beginning because he included David and Melissa in just about everything we did, such as finding out the best July 4th fireworks location and planning picnics and fishing trips. I'll never forget David's excitement when he caught his first fish.

I met Richard's family on one of those picnics in the mountains. David, Melissa, and I watched the banter between his mom and dad, his sisters and their husbands, and all of those nieces and nephews. Suddenly, it hit me: the family I had yearned for was right before my eyes. It was hard to keep from crying. Then I had one consuming thought. *If I lose this guy, I'm gonna die.*

Well, I didn't die. Richard asked me to marry him, and I was on cloud nine. Each day convinced me more and more that this man was something special. Richard was handsome, kind, hardworking, faithful—and such a gentleman. I knew he was going to take care of us, and he had a family I wanted to be part of. I just knew this marriage was going to be different.

We were going to have the perfect family.

Our wedding was beautiful and everything a bride could want. We enjoyed our honeymoon in San Francisco. Driving up the coast with my new husband in his metallic silver Corvette Stingray, I felt like I was in a movie. Have you ever ridden in a Corvette? I had to keep pinching myself. It was a wonderful honeymoon and a special promise of things to come.

Richard adopted David and Melissa. Our daughter Jennifer was two when I was pregnant with our son Andrew. By now we lived in Alpine, a San Diego suburb, in a quaint mountain community in a little house behind our family business.

Life Isn't Always Rosy

By the way, I forgot to tell you what the family business was. We owned a liquor store. Yes, that was the business of Richard's parents. They bought a liquor store for us to manage, and we knew one day it would be our own. I had quit my job at the telephone company, and now I worked alongside Richard at the store.

You can make a lot of money in the liquor business. We were financially secure, and again this should have been the place in the story when we all lived happily ever after. But that wasn't going to happen.

When Andrew was only four months old, one day I found myself sitting in my living room, crying, and wondering, *What's wrong with me?* I knew I should have been the happiest woman on earth. Richard hadn't changed, our four children were happy, and we were healthy. We enjoyed tremendous security in our business, and I was part of a family that was all I had ever hoped for.

Yet it wasn't enough. My family and the financial security hadn't given me peace or happiness. I had no confidence or joy, and my life was empty. I was scared to death, but I didn't even know why. Worse, I had begun drinking just like my mom. Little by little alcohol had crept into my life until I didn't want to do without it. And let me tell you, if you're going to drink, a liquor store is the business to be in. My life was disintegrating right before my eyes, and I didn't know what to do. I felt helpless.

Valuable Friends

When I worked at the telephone company, I had met a girl named Edna. From the beginning we connected. Both of us were outgoing, independent, and boisterous.

Our childhoods had even been similar. We were tough, and boy did that toughness show in our language. We told each other the best dirty jokes, and Edna was my drinking buddy.

I missed Edna when I quit the phone company, and then she moved away. But it was about this time that she called to say that she'd just moved back and wanted to invite me over to her house for lunch. I thought, *This is my answer. Edna will help me get back on track.*

But as soon as I walked in her door, I knew something was different. She didn't tell one dirty joke, and she didn't laugh at the things she'd laughed at before. She didn't offer me a beer, and I never heard one bad word come out of her mouth.

What's happened to her? I wondered.

During lunch I told her about my unhappiness and depression. She listened to me quietly, nodded, and smiled. This was not the Edna I remembered. I must admit that I was confused. Edna possessed a quiet confidence, a sense of peace that unsettled me. I left her house that day, wondering if we could still be friends.

A few days later she called me and invited me to church. Now, the last thing I wanted to do was go to church. Church had never done a thing for me, and I had every excuse you could think of not to go.

"I really can't go, Edna," I told her. "Richard works on Sundays, Andrew is just a baby, and I don't have a car."

But she was stubborn. "Church is at nine. There's a nursery for Andrew and classes for your kids. Our van is big enough for all of us. We'll pick you up at 8:30. Just be ready."

Edna may have changed, but one thing was certain. That girl hadn't lost her aggressive nature. I went to church.

Transformation

The last Sunday that month was January 27th. I don't remember what the whole message was about that day, but I do remember what the minister said at the end. We were standing and about to sing a closing hymn when he asked if some wanted to give up their search for peace and ask the Lord Jesus to come into their hearts. It struck me that all my life I'd been searching for peace and happiness, for the perfect family. *Nothing* had filled that emptiness or taken away my fear. I had tried everything I knew.

This church was different than those I had attended before. Now I heard the truth about life, heaven, and real love. It was a different experience from what I had ever known. I learned about God, who is a personal God. I learned that He's interested in *me*!

After the service Edna and I talked, and I learned more. Sure, I had heard about Jesus' death on the cross, *but I hadn't known that He died for me*. She told me, "For God so loved the world [that means you, Judy], that He gave His only begotten Son, that whoever believes in Him shall not perish, but have eternal life."[15]

I had never understood that I was sinful and separated from God. Oh, I knew what guilt felt like—that was part of my problem—but I didn't know what to do about it. Like a lot of people, I just hoped that the good things I had done, such as volunteering at a hospital, giving to charity, or fixing a meal for my neighbor, would *outweigh* the bad stuff, such as talking bad about someone, fudging on my taxes, or lying to my boss.

Those are just little things, I thought. *They don't amount to much, do they?*

I had heard that God is good. I had heard that He is kind! *If that's really true*, I thought, *then He'll balance those things out and let me into heaven, won't He?*

The Bible says, "...for all have sinned and fall short of the glory of God."[16] We harbor resentment and fight jealousy and pride. We're selfish and stubborn. Some of us are angry and bitter. "For the wages of sin is death [separation from God], but the free gift of God is eternal life through Christ Jesus our Lord."[17] This was news to me and it certainly explained my fear of death.

"But God showed his great love for us by sending Christ to die for us while we were still sinners."[18] He paid the penalty for my sin, and He is the only one who could have done that.

In all my years of going to church with my grandma and then by myself, I had *never once heard* that I must individually receive Jesus Christ as my Savior and Lord. The Bible says, "But to all who believed him and accepted him, he gave the right to become children of God."[19] This was wonderful news to me. It answered some of my questions, such as "How can I be good?" and "How can I be sure I'm going to heaven?"

Because I wanted the peace the minister had talked about, I prayed and asked Jesus into my life. There were no fireworks, but I remember the peace that flooded over me. It was like one of my grandma's quilts wrapped around me. I knew something good had happened. I had surrendered my life to Jesus, and now He was in control, not me. He was in charge of my security, not me. Now I had Someone who would love me no matter what, and I had found the peace I had always longed for.

It was weird, but now I *wanted* to go to church, and Edna didn't seem so strange anymore. God began to change me, and I was making better choices and acting differently. My kids noticed, my husband noticed, and a year or so later he also asked Jesus into his heart. One by one Jesus came into all of their lives, including my mom and dad, but that's another story I'll tell later.

We got out of the liquor business, and Richard began a career as an aerospace engineer. We also had two more babies, and being a mom kept me busy for several years. When my youngest began school, I became a public school librarian and worked at that for fifteen years.

Retirement was within our reach, and boy did we have some big plans! We were healthy and energetic (well, that depends on what time of day it was), and we longed for the day when we would be able to take off for parts unknown. When I saw a jetliner streaking across the sky, I thought, *One day we're going to be on one of those.* Our oldest daughter and her family lived and worked in Africa, and that was the first place we planned to visit.

Big Changes Ahead

But eleven years ago my dear Richard had that massive stroke I mentioned earlier. It was so disabling that the ER nurse told me to call my family because she didn't think he would survive. I watched helplessly as the doctors worked to save his life. They asked me to make decisions about things I knew nothing about. I didn't even know the difference between a stroke and a heart attack. I sure do now, but then I was scared to death and couldn't think straight. I simply said, "Lord, I don't know what to do, but I know I trust You."

Later, in the ICU I sat at Richard's side around the clock. He couldn't move, and he couldn't talk, but those blue eyes seemed alert. I asked him, "Honey, I have to know. Are you still with me?"

His right arm moved slowly across the blanket, and he gave me a thumbs-up!

I was overcome with such joy and encouragement. *He understood me!* I cradled his head and whispered, "This is the sickness part isn't it, sweetheart?"

It had never dawned on me when we were driving along in that Corvette so many years ago that those vows we had just made ("In sickness and in health, for better or for worse, till death do us part") might come to something like this. We cried that night, but without a doubt, I felt God's presence in that room and it comforted us.

Against all odds, my Richard survived, and we retired, but not like we expected. After eight weeks in the hospital, we came home to a whole new life.

Richard sits in a wheelchair and is paralyzed on his left side, but his speech returned, which is a major miracle we are so thankful for. His right side works fine, so he can eat, and he can stand when he's moving from his wheelchair to his favorite easy chair. Right after we got home from the hospital, a beautiful lift chair was delivered to our door from an anonymous donor. It is Richard's favorite chair, and he actually couldn't live without it. Thank you from the bottom of our hearts, whoever you are.

We've had to give up some things, but we try to keep our lives as normal as possible. For example, we walk on the beach. Once we were at San Clemente, and I wanted to get Richard's wheelchair down by the water. Now, this was before I knew about those wheelchairs with the big balloon tires you can borrow at the beach.

I took a look at the beach and thought, *I can do this*. I got a running start, hit that sand, and almost shot Richard into the ocean like a bullet. Poor guy! The things he has to put up with! His next birthday gifts are going to be a seat belt and a helmet.

Richard needs me to do things he used to do for himself, but I discovered something wonderful. I enjoy caring for him. I want to do whatever I can to make his life easier. But even this lifestyle can be challenging. For example, I have to sit on the floor in front of him to put the brace on his left leg and his shoes and socks on.

One morning when I got down on the floor, my knees cracked, and my back groaned. I said, "Honey, I'm sixty-seven now. What's this going to be like when I'm eighty?"

We both know that one of these days, I'll get down and stay there. But you know what? I'll worry about that later.

How About You?

You know, my joy, my peace, and my abilities are not natural. Listen, life isn't always rosy at our house. We have our ups and downs just like everyone else does. Some days we get discouraged, but I can say this with confidence: when you ask Jesus to come into your life and heart and make you new, He will do it. That's His promise.

And now I have questions for you. Do you want your life to change? Are you interested in finding peace and security and joy, like I was? Your circumstances may not change, but I guarantee that your heart will.

Intellectually agreeing that Jesus is the Son of God and that He died on the cross for our sins and rose from the dead is not enough. We must receive Him by faith as an act of our own wills. The Bible says, "If you confess with your mouth that Jesus is Lord and believe in your heart that God raised him from the dead, you will be saved."[20]

Whether you're young or old, God sends the same message to each of us. Maybe you're thinking it's too late to change, or maybe you have misunderstood, just like I did, who Jesus is and what He has done.

I want to ask you this: Are you hurting? Are you weary? Are you in despair over the way your life has gone? Have you searched everywhere, like I did? Maybe you think your problems are too difficult to overcome, and you feel helpless and hopeless like I did so many years ago.

But you know what? As long as you're living and breathing, it's not too late. I was thirty-one when I asked the Lord for forgiveness and eternal life. And just look what He's done for me! The Bible says, "What this means is that those who become Christians become new persons. They are not the same anymore, for the old life is gone. A new life has begun!" [21]

I'm a new person—there's no doubt about it. It's been over thirty years since I've had any alcohol to drink. I have no desire for it at all. And right away God showed me that a child of His doesn't talk the way I did.

I would never have made those changes on my own. It took a while, but now I have a clue how to love and support my husband. And I have the joy of nurturing and cherishing my six kids, five of whom are married. Their spouses are like having five more kids, and then we have thirteen grandchildren. And guess what? It's the perfect family, the one I was always searching for. God is the One who makes perfect families.

Jesus changed my life, and He'll change yours too. All you have to do is ask Him.

Here's an opportunity for you to do just that. Below is a brief prayer. If you would like to turn your life over to Jesus and begin a personal relationship with Him, it's very simple. Find a quiet spot and—with an honest and sincere heart—pray this prayer.

Lord Jesus, I want to thank You for dying on the cross to save me from my sin. Thank You that You rose again, and thank You for the place in heaven You have made for me. Forgive me for my sin. Forgive me for excluding You from my life. Would You come into my heart and make me brand new too? Thank You for Your gift of eternal life and for Your Holy Spirit, who has now come to live inside me. Amen.

If you just prayed that prayer for the first time and really meant it, I have some good news. What happened to me over thirty-five years ago has just happened to you. You are now God's child, a part of His perfect family. You are forgiven, and you will spend eternity in heaven. Dear one, your future is secure, and the best news is that God can help you change. He can meet any need you have in your life. And no matter what life throws your way, you will never go through it alone. I can promise you that, because I'm living proof.

My dear woman, this book has been a testimony of how God has worked in my life. I want to repeat what I told you before. I haven't gone into great detail, but let me remind you of what I mentioned earlier.

I came from a dysfunctional, broken family. I was a young, confused, and frightened girl who had young, confused, and frightened alcoholic parents. I was a high school dropout, an unwed mother, and a teenage wife and mom. I was divorced and on my way to becoming a full-blown alcoholic. This tough and coarse-talking young woman had been around the block. You don't need sordid details. The important part is that God changed me.

More than anything I want you to see that I'm like most of you—normal. I have no fancy claim to fame, nor do I have any exceptional aptitudes. Yet God has taken my life and made it exceptional. He's just waiting to do that for you too. Will you take Him up on it today? God bless you as you seek to keep your family secure in this shaky world.

After reading this book, if you prayed that prayer or you have questions or comments, please contact me at judyscharf@ verizon.net. I eagerly look forward to hearing from you, and I promise: you will receive an answer.

Web Sites to Help You Keep Your Family Secure

http://www.flylady.net
Just fifteen minutes are all it takes to simpli-FLY your life!

http://www.savingdinner.com
Menu Planning Solutions

http://www.cheapskatemonthly.com
Debt-Free Living and Other Tips

http://www.daveramsey.com
Life, Money, Hope

http://www.mulberrylanefarm.com
You can taste the difference.

http://www.emiliebarnes.com
More Hours in My Day

www.the-cutting-edge.org
The Victory Bible Reading Plan for the whole family.

ENDNOTES

1. Sally Field, "Interview with Sally Field", *Good House-keeping Magazine*, March 2009, Page 137.
2. www.slate.com
3. *Family First*, by Dr. Phil McGraw, Free Press, a division of Simon and Schuster, 2004, Page 51.
4. 1921–1994. William Arthur Ward was an American author, editor, pastor, and teacher. His quotes are both motivating and inspiring.
5. *John Newton: The Angry Sailor* by Kay Marshall Strom, Moody Press, Chicago, 1984.
6. Reader's Digest Best Loved Books for Young Readers, Volume Two, copyright 1966, The Reader's Digest Association, Pleasantville, New York, The Scarlet Pimpernel by Baroness Orczy, Page 9.
7. Philippians 2:3–4.
8. Rosemary Ellis, Editor-in-Chief, "On My Mind" Editor's Letter, *Good Housekeeping Magazine*, August 2008, Page 15.

9. Dr. William F. Fry, Nevada City, CA, Permission to use quote given via phone call on 8-10-2009.
10. Loma Linda University School of Medicine News, Fall 1999, www.llu.edu, News and Events.
11. Dr. Robert Sallis, "Get Off Your Seat", Partners in Health Magazine, Kaiser Permanente, Fall, 2008, F.I.T.T. Principle, Page 9.
12. Judith Scharfenberg, *Rest Stops for Busy Moms*, "*Summer and Blue Eyes*" Page 25, Nashville: Broadman & Holman Publishers, copyright 2003, Judith Scharfenberg.
13. "O Love That Wilt Not Let Me Go," lyrics by George Matheson, published in 1882.
14. Dr. Phil Daily Television Program on CBS, various air times.
15. John 3:16.
16. Romans 3:23.
17. Romans 6:23 (NLT).
18. Romans 5:8 (NLT).
19. John 1:12 (NLT).
20. Romans 10:9 (NLT).
21. 2 Corinthians 5:17 (NLT).